ACTING
FOR FILM

CATHY HAASE

ALLWORTH PRESS
NEW YORK

08 07 06 05 04 03   5 4 3 2 1

Published by Allworth Press
An imprint of Allworth Communications, Inc.
10 East 23rd Street, New York, NY 10010

Front cover photo by Tom Zuback:
John Gallagher directs Heather Matarazzo and Brian Vincent in *The Deli*.
From the collection of John Gallagher

Cover design by Mary Belibasakis

Page composition/typography by Integra Software Services, Pvt. Ltd., Pondicherry, India

ISBN: 1-58115-252-3

Library of Congress Cataloging-in-Publication Data

Haase, Cathy.
Acting for film / Cathy Haase.
  p. cm.
Includes bibliographical references and index.
ISBN 1-58115-252-3
1. Motion picture acting. I. Title.

PN1995.9.A26 H33 2003
792'.028–dc21
2002014956
Printed in Canada

ACKNOWLEDGMENTS

This book would not have been possible without my work with the great teacher, Walter Lott.

I would like to thank the following people for their support, advice, and sharing their knowledge: Ulla Zwicker; John Woodward; Marilyn Moore; Leslie Kaminoff; Leonard Easter; Marilyn Horowitz; Patch Schwadron; my editor, Nicole Potter, and publisher Tad Crawford of Allworth Press; all of my students; and the School of Visual Arts, especially the film chairman Reeves Lehmann. A special acknowledgement must go to my husband, Steve Thurston, for his patience, understanding, and loving support, for which I am forever grateful.

WHERE AM I COMING FROM?

Acting for Film is a book about acting in motion pictures and the techniques that can be used to act in front of the camera. It's written to the actor, which is what I am, and discloses some of the approaches to film acting that have been prevalent in American movies. Being an actor, I have a very practical, yet personal approach to things. Whatever the technique or philosophy is, it has to work for me in the field; it has to work when the camera is rolling. Every actor is a unique instrument that only he or she knows how to play, so my advice to you is, take everything in, keep what works for you, and leave the rest for later.

Many people think that film acting is simply a portrayal of a strong personality, that the actor, who possesses a strong ego and a love of performing, just memorizes the lines and jumps before the camera. People think that it takes a certain type of personality to do this, and it does, but what they don't consider are the intricate techniques of craft that the actor practices and the depth of self-knowledge that she must strive for in developing her instrument. In today's American entertainment industry of buff bodies and beautiful faces, it's easy to see how the public could think that a couple of sit-ups and high cheekbones create a movie legend. This idea is so prevalent that it even exists among the acting community itself. In order to get jobs that will pay the rent, everyone hits the gym, has facials, does workshops on selling themselves, and studies comedy improv. The actor as commodity is a reality in our world, and although there's nothing wrong with any of these activities, they won't create a foundation of technique. What about the gymnasium of the soul? What about the quest for self-knowledge? Where does one learn to illuminate the actions of the character with greater truths that will touch an audience forever?

I believe that actors need to build a strong personal, private relationship between themselves and their creative instrument, which they can access for the characters they play regardless of the style or medium they are working in. This work has to accompany all of the other rules of acting, like finding the intentions and needs of the character, the actions and beats of the scene, and the analysis and memorization of the script. Film acting presents some special problems for those trained solely in the theater, and I will try, whenever possible, to discuss how one can adjust a theatrical technique for work in front of the camera. For many who dream of acting in film, the available education is too theatrically oriented to allow them to fully blossom as film actors. This book speaks to both those with theater training and those entering the field for the first time as film actors.

Strangely enough, although this is a book about acting in film, in my classes, I never employ the camera itself as a way of aiding an actor to develop a film acting technique. Certainly, there are things that you can learn from watching yourself on camera, and I deal with what I think those things are in the last chapter of this book. Mostly, I feel that bringing the camera into the classroom creates a misleading image. First, the camera image will more than likely be primitive and simple. It won't provide a true representation of what an actor will look and be like in a professional film. Using a camera in the classroom as an acting tool takes the focus away from watching the actor and brings the attention to the television monitor. Second, since many of my students are young people who have spent their lives watching television and computer screens, I feel it is important to teach them to watch and observe themselves and one another, rather than relying on a video image inside yet another box.

THE ACTORS STUDIO

I am a member of the Actors Studio, where I have had the privilege of working with and watching many of the great actors and acting teachers of the twentieth century. I originally learned this work—and it's usually referred to as just that, "the work"—from Walter Lott, who was my teacher for many years. Walter was a prodigy of Lee Strasberg, and he worked with all of the other renowned teachers of that time, notably Sandy Meisner, Bobby Lewis, and Stella Adler. So, it is through Walter that I learned many of the things upon which I would then base my own teaching.

Walter was a great and ominous presence in all of his student's lives. He possessed a passion for "the work" that was unrelenting in his belief in the actor's power to represent truth, not only personal truth in a specific moment, but a greater truth for mankind. Wherever he taught, and he taught all over the world, he instilled each and every student with the belief that his or her acting instrument, if connected to the truth, was a vehicle of expression that was very important to be seen and heard. Was it true? I don't know, but I do know that it is the only way that an artist can work. It is certainly the only way that an actor can work in front of the camera. You have to work with the belief that what you are doing is important, you must be committed to a sense of your own personal truth, and you must engage in a practice that will bring these things to life in the script and character.

A NOTE TO TEACHERS

I think that the saying, "Those who can do, those who can't teach," is a great misrepresentation of teaching, especially in the arts, and perhaps in all fields. A better way of putting it would be, "Those that do it the best have a responsibility to teach." All acting teachers that I know who are worth their salt are excellent actors in their own right, and therefore, this book is written for teachers as well. If you are unfamiliar with the techniques, particularly in the first section of the book, then I would suggest only using them after you have explored them through the filters of your own acting technique. They can unleash a wave of creative power that you have to be prepared to guide your students through. The only way you'll be able to do that is through your own personal experience.

I teach a course at the School of Visual Arts called Acting for Film, on which this book is loosely based. The students who I teach are first-year aspiring filmmakers, and they are required to study acting as part of their curriculum. They are often unwilling participants, having thought that opting for a career behind the camera would excuse them from experiencing what happens in front of it. It never ceases to amaze me that once they have been taught to be in contact with their own inner lives through the relaxation, they can be taught to express that inner life through the senses. Then, through a character and text, many of them discover a talent that they didn't know they had, and they continue to study acting.

Acting in front of the camera has widened the field of people who could possibly be actors. You no longer need a large voice or gregarious personality to get out there on the stage to be seen and heard. The camera has privatized acting to enclose a much smaller circle that is concentrated closer to the person playing the part, rather than the part itself. I mention this to teachers, because there might be students in your class who desperately want to act, but are too shy to project outward and perform. It's possible that their voice is so soft that it cannot be heard, and although they do their best work sotto voce, they are still compelling to watch. These students can be very frustrating, but they shouldn't be left by the wayside; they might have the makings of very good film actors.

THE BOOK

This book is divided into three parts. The first part, The Actor, deals with exercises of relaxation, concentration, and sense memory. It is by no means complete; such a book would have to be at least the size of a bible, because like the bible, many different people would have to contribute to the story. Sense memory, for example, is a very personal issue that works differently for each person who uses it. I have presented a framework that you can spring from through personal practice and further study. The material is presented directly to actors working on their own, although if you find that you would like to truly explore the possibilities of sense memory, you should find a class with an excellent teacher to complete the study.

The second part of the book, The Script and Character Development, begins to take the actor out into the world of working in films. I cover the audition and casting process by giving you the information that you need to function at your best. This section will help you use the screenplay format to glean clues to the character, as well as guide you in preparing for the shoot, once you have a part to play in a film.

In the last section of the book, The Shoot, I attempt to equip you with a knowledge of filmmaking and the processes that go into it that are important for the actor. The pros and cons of participating in the various levels of student films are also discussed in this section. I then create a hypothetical film shoot and your first day on the set and suggest ways of using "the work" to do what is expected of you. Lastly comes the suggestion to learn to be an objective observer of your work when you watch your own image on the screen and to learn how to grow from the experience.

I find myself asking myself many questions as I move through my life as an actor and an acting teacher. Does the dream of the movies as a powerful medium of change still exist beyond the popcorn and surround-sound of mindless entertainment? I enjoy the entertainment along with the millions at the movie theaters—I love movies of all kinds—but I keep searching for the films that expand the meaning in my life. I keep going back to the ones that have done it for me in the past, and I keep searching for the new ones that will do it for me now. I keep wondering, Can we, as actors, hold our human integrity and portray humanity in a way that gives meaning to our lives and to the lives of others? I believe that we can if we desire to do so. It's a choice that every actor has to make, and every actor meets his or her decision differently through the pathways of life.

A few months into writing this book, I found out that Walter Lott had passed away at his home in Chicago. I hadn't seen him for several years, and I'd been thinking about calling to talk over my writing project. He had always wanted to write a book, often having me take notes at his workshops for him, notes that he would invariably leave on a café table somewhere in Berlin. With Walter, it was always about the further exploration of the moment, the deeper investigation of the feeling, moving forward, asking questions, teaching, observing, living. He just never found the time to put it all down on paper. So, here I sit, his pupil, writing, teaching, taking what I could from him, which was a great deal, and from all the other teachers of my life, and filtering it through my own acting instrument and experience. I have learned as much from my students as they have learned from me, and so it goes; it never ends.

PART ONE

THE ACTOR

RELAXATION AND THE ART OF THE FACE

Close your eyes and allow the movie in your mind to travel through the land of your favorite film images. Don't try to remember a title or a specific movie and then search for the image. Allow your mind's eye a free hand, and sit back and enjoy the show. Films from childhood, cartoons, adventures, love scenes, swells of music, and magnificent landscapes will dance in your imagination, but more than anything, there will be faces. Faces looking out at you telling you their stories through their expressions. Faces of famous actors, and faces of unknowns. Faces in the crowd. Faces of children, of old people, of nymphs and heroes. Whatever they look like, whoever they are, they will all have one thing in common. They will all be beautiful. They are beautiful because they have touched you in a special way that has become part of the fabric of your identity. This relationship you have with the movie images in your mind is a very intimate one. It is, in fact, a love relationship, and being such, it is a very complex and volatile affair. It's best to embrace this relationship right at the beginning, as you begin to think about yourself within those movie images and see your own face among them.

One's relationship to one's own face is something that most people have thought about to varying degrees. It comes in the guise of how you feel about your looks, whether you think you are attractive or ugly or sexy or whatever. Some people think about it a lot, others hardly at all, but most people do not occupy themselves with their relationship to their faces in the manner or form of a movie actor. The face and how it functions for the individual is paramount to the film actor. It goes way beyond the realm of looks. This is a relationship as passionate as any love affair, as spiritual as god, and as lasting as a mother to her child. When people speak of the vanity and introspection of actors, they have no idea how meager this terminology is.

That being said, you must not look at this relationship as a negative one. You must see it as a tool of the craft that you would like to pursue. The way you look, and beyond that the quality you project on screen, determines the parts that you play. It's as simple as that. There is room for everyone on the screen, as your own favorite reel of movie memories will tell you. Not everyone is a bathing beauty. Some of the more indelible types have been profoundly strange-looking, sad, or old. Wherever you fit into this wide spectrum of human looks, if you want to be a film actor, you must learn to accept yourself (or the struggle that you face in attempting to do that) and freely interact with yourself through your feelings. This interaction is seen, through relaxation, on the expression it releases in the muscles of your face. The work the actor puts into trying to perfect this interaction, which begins with the self and then extends to the character, the script, the other actor, etc., begins with the Mental Relaxation exercises. They seem very simple, and they are. It is here, with these simple structures, that one can begin building the "muscles" that, like an athlete, you will need to be a film actor.

MENTAL RELAXATION

Sit in a chair. An ordinary metal folding chair is good or any sturdy, straight-backed chair with no arms and no cushions. Have a clock nearby, so you can time yourself. In the beginning, give yourself twenty minutes. At first, just try and breathe calmly and fully with closed eyes. Try and take the pressure off. Unlike yoga or meditation, where you are told to always go back to the mantra and remain calm, these exercises are geared to bring you more in touch with how you feel and what's going on with you at that very moment. You must try and remain present. You must try not to retreat into a dreamlike state or shut down completely and feel nothing. As human beings, we are living and feeling all the time. Actors are professional feelers. The trick is to learn how to feel many complex things and to remain relaxed. This is true of all acting, but it is particularly true of film acting, where the camera reads everything and the actor is often confined to little or no movement.

It is too late to start getting used to being relaxed, but alive in front of the camera when you have a job or are at an audition. The work towards Mental Relaxation should be part of a daily practice, like exercise or the scales of a musician. Actors work simply and diligently against their mortal enemy, tension. Certainly, there's plenty of tension on a movie set, and the actor's face in varying degrees of close-up is often the target of everyone's attention. Therefore, the actor must be prepared to face the cameras for long periods of time, often being asked to do the same things over and over again, without becoming tense and tired. The muscles of the face must be trained to withstand this marathon of expression. They must be trained before you get to the set.

1 Sit in a chair, keeping your back straight, your head balancing straight on the top of the spine, feet flat on the floor, arms either on top of your lap with palms down or hanging at your sides, and your eyes closed.

2 Just breathe, letting the air come high into the chest, so that the rib cage and breastbone move with each inhalation and exhalation. Don't let the air fall into the stomach area. Keep it in the upper chest.

3 Open your mouth slightly, so that the teeth are not touching. This is actually releasing the jaw.

4 Sigh three of four times without moving the head around or fidgeting. Just sit and breathe, and sigh without moving.

5 Concentrate on your eyes. Imagine that the eyes are two soft pools of clear, calm water. Check for twitching or furrowing of the brow. If you find tension around the eyes, release it with a sigh or a deep breath. Make sure that no other part of your body is moving, that your jaw is released, and your breath is high in the chest and steady. Throughout the Mental Relaxation exercises, keep checking for ways that the tension escapes to other parts of the body, like feet that curl around the legs of the chair, or hands that suddenly grab the seat, or eyelids that uncontrollably flutter. Keep checking for tension, and release it, while concentrating on the eyeballs themselves.

6 Now, lift the eyeballs up as high as you can, while keeping the lids closed. You should feel the stretch of the tendons around the eyes. Do not lift the head up or bend it downwards, but try and keep it straight and easy as you keep the eyes lifted. Keep breathing and sighing, and hold for twenty seconds. Don't lock the jaw. Then, release the eyes to their normal position.

7 Stretch the eyes to the left, and hold them there for ten seconds. Release them to their normal position. Repeat to the right. Stretch them down towards the tip of the nose. Hold for ten seconds and release.

Relaxation and the Art of the Face

8 At this point, check for signs of rising tension anywhere in the body, particularly in the face, head, neck, and shoulder region. The eyelids remain closed, but an inner eye is vigilantly at work keeping all the instructions in order. A small, quiet invisible director inside the mind's eye is investigating.

9 Now, rotate the eyes to all extreme positions. Up, right, down, left, up, right, down, left, etc. Try to breathe normally, keeping the jaw released and the head still, as you stretch the eyes as far as you can in each position, rotating to the next. Do about five rotations.

10 Now, rotate the eyes in the opposite direction, up, left, down, right, etc., and repeat about five rotations.

Whenever you are repeating something in the opposite direction, on the other side, or just repeating a series, approach it as if it were the first time you had ever done it. Approach it as if it were a new adventure of discovery, and avoid feeling secure and familiar. This is a very important aspect of the work. It is training the muscles to always find new things, to be in a perpetual state of discovery, even though an action has been repeated many times.

NOTE ABOUT THE EXERCISES: All of the following exercises will follow the same format as I described above. The sitting position in the chair, the posture, and the investigation of random movement and tension should all be maintained while doing the specific movements. The general motto is: "Don't get bored, don't get stiff, just keep investigating."

MENTAL RELAXATION EXERCISE #2

1 Concentrate on your eyebrows. Raise them up and bring them down. Move up and down as quickly as you can. Repeat this motion in rapid succession for about ten seconds, and then stop to rest. Then, repeat it again.

2 Try to do the same movement with the eyebrows, only this time incorporate the entire skin of the scalp, so that it too moves back and forth. Repeat a series, rest, and do it again.

3 Squinch the face together, as if you had an extreme lemon reaction, and hold for a few seconds, then release. Repeat five times.

4 Spread the mouth in a thin, wide, tense smile, then quickly draw the lips together in a tight, round kiss position. Go back and forth between the two positions.

5 Concentrate on the upper lip. Tap it with your fingers. Pinch it and pull it into different directions. Now, without using your hands, imagine that the upper lip is divided into two segments like the mouth of a bunny. See if you can move the two sides independent of one another. Try to do this and breathe at the same time.

6 Now, pull the lips over the teeth like you were pretending to be toothless. Open and close the mouth, while stretching the lips over the teeth and releasing.

7 Now, do a combination of all of the above movements and incorporate the eyes, moving freely from one type of movement to the other. Don't forget to breathe!

At this point, let's take stock of what's happening while we're doing the exercises. For each person, the experience will be different, but for everyone, as you move the muscles of the face, different thoughts and feelings will be unleashed. Our faces do a lot of work for us. They are our shields from the rest of the world, a thin dividing line between them and us. Our faces are riddled with defenses that protect us in our daily lives, usually concealing what we really feel. Now is the time to bring those defenses down and let the face and feelings interact freely, without regard for social protocol. Don't judge yourself or get caught in trying to figure something out. Just keep moving. Keep moving forward.

It is important to "move forward" during these relaxation exercises in order to achieve a state of active relaxation. As one works, the meaning of the phrase "move forward" becomes clearer. This is a state in which you are always actively discovering and investigating something new. The word "relaxation," especially when applied to a mental state, is often related to a feeling of repose, of calm, and of harmony. This is a different type of endeavor, very different from what the actor needs at this point in the work. Later on, when one is battling nerves, many of the same exercises can be used to achieve a state of calm; however, at this juncture, we are trying to create an atmosphere of productive conflict, rather than that of harmony and peace. It is safe to say that we are trying to achieve an active state of conflict between the inside (the feelings, thoughts, and memories, etc.) and the outside (the expressions of the face, body movements, and the voice) of the actor. The first step in doing this it to incorporate the voice as part of the Mental Relaxation.

Talking and speech also take place on the face and cause a lot of problems in film acting. This isn't the same problem of vocal projection that occurs on stage, but the problem of connection to the words. Film is very intimate; it's public privacy with the audience as potential voyeurs sitting out there somewhere in the future. Speech must occur with subtle and full expression within the confines of the all-exposing close-up. Therefore, at this time, it is important to start incorporating the voice as a mechanism of releasing tension and deepening the relaxation process. If the vocal mechanism is not brought in as part of the relaxation at this very beginning point, I feel it always lags behind. An actor who neglects training the vocal aspects of the talent will always be able to *emote* more than he or she will be able to communicate through sound and language. This can be a disadvantage to an actor.

GIBBERISH

A speech teacher of mine once said that speaking is an *ahhhh* sound with the articulation of the mouth, tongue, and lips. I remember thinking, "Oh, that's easy—I can do that, no problem." I'm still trying to do it. What *we're* going to try and do is not to speak, per se, but to make sounds by moving the mouth, tongue, and lips vigorously, while connecting to our thoughts. In other words, we're going to speak *Gibberish. Webster's* dictionary describes gibberish as rapid and inarticulate talk, unintelligible chatter, jargon, unmeaning, unintelligible, incoherent. All very comforting words for those about to let their defenses down and express their innermost thoughts. The idea is to connect to the mental impulse without thinking and express it directly through the sounds and movements of Gibberish. You should try and keep the head easy and free and the body still. The sounds, however, could be anything and vary in volume. Don't try to make the sounds fit what you think you're feeling, but rather, allow the sounds of Gibberish to inform and surprise you.

MENTAL RELAXATION EXERCISE #3

Still sitting in the chair as before, do the facial acrobatics of exercises #1 and #2, while doing Gibberish. Make sure you inhale and exhale fully. The deeper you investigate the relaxation, the more air you need, so don't forget to breathe. This exercise can be done with the eyes open, however, if it's more difficult to concentrate, keep them closed for now.

Putting the movements of the eyes and face together with the Gibberish is a multitask action. It's doing several things at once. If you find yourself having trouble with all of this and feeling like a fool, just work on completing the tasks to the fullest of your ability. In this way, you increase your commitment to fulfilling the requirements of the exercise each time you do it. When the exercise is simple, it's an excellent time to work on concentration and commitment. It takes confidence to accomplish tasks that make you feel silly, and any feelings of doubt or self-consciousness should be expressed through the Gibberish.

When I was shooting one of the last scenes in *The Ballad of Little Jo* on location in Montana, I had a serious attack of absurdity just before we were about to shoot. There we were, a few of the remaining old-timers sitting around a table in my saloon, all aged to our seventies with latex, wigs, and makeup. When they'd finished doing my makeup, I couldn't believe how much I looked like my mother, and it frightened me. It also gave me an insight into the movement of the character, and I was very engrossed, so I was completely taken by surprise by my silly attack. With the naked eye, you could see the theatrical contrivance of our costuming: the bits of glue on the moustache, a visible web of a wig, the cautious, careful staining of our clothes to make them look old and worn and country-like. All this would read authentic to the camera, but in the few moments before shooting, it suddenly seemed absurd to me. Need I mention that it was a very serious scene, and one in which I was to be nearly on the verge of tears, lost in remembrances of things long past, and all I could think about was that my corset was too tight and I thought this was a really stupid thing for an adult to do—dress up and pretend.

As an actor, I had to acknowledge how I felt. I even mentioned it to my fellow actors, in character and in her slow twangy voice: "This is a really dumb thing to do with your life." And they all nodded and mumbled and took the opportunity to scratch their beards, but then it was time to shoot, and the concentration had to be directed to the task at hand, and everything else went into the performance. Playing old requires tremendous relaxation, because the movements tend to be slower and the muscles hang differently, and therefore, achieving a realistic physicality requires tremendous concentration and commitment. If your instrument is trained to keep the commitment in the simplest of exercises, it will be there for you when you need it at crucial moments like the one I just described.

The mind may wander to many different places or thoughts while you're doing these exercises. How you feel about yourself and what you are doing may surface at this moment. It isn't your job at this point to try and figure out why such and such is happening or what it means. It is only your job to be aware that it is happening. The dilemma of all actors, and particularly the screen actor, is that we must be aware of what we are doing in the moment we are doing it. We must be able to identify the impulse without thinking much about it. This is the beginning of the moment-to-moment acting reality that whispers across the landscape of the face.

THE INNER MONOLOGUE

It is inevitable that the Gibberish eventually becomes words. Actors are always worrying about the words. Do I have to learn the words? Will I remember the words? What do the words mean? And so on. At this point in the game, the words don't matter. The only important thing is that the words be directly connected to what you are thinking or feeling in the moment. Uncensored, not-thought-out, inexplicable words and sentences that comprise the Inner Monologue.

In my classes, I usually suggest that people move from the Gibberish into the Inner Monologue in a whisper. I tell my students to use private, intimate speech that is barely audible, if at all. "Nobody cares what you're saying anyway. Just try and get someone to really listen to you, and you'll see," I tell them. "Everyone is too concerned with his or her own dramas and dilemmas to care about you. So, dive in, go ahead and speak to yourself out loud." It doesn't seem to make it any easier that I'm asking the whole class to speak at once in a sort of crazy cacophony of sound without any regard for who is listening. It's very difficult to speak your private thoughts out loud; just try doing it alone, and you'll see how hard it is. Usually, you have to shift back and forth between the Gibberish and the Inner Monologue to keep the thought process going and not get stuck in your head. Even the students who are doing this exercise in a mother tongue no one else in the class can understand are reticent and struggle to express themselves. So, you see, the words themselves don't really matter at this point. It is the privacy of the expression that is difficult to reveal. The more private and intimate the feeling, the greater the need for relaxation.

It is through the doing of these exercises over a period of time that their true value becomes clear. You should start with twenty to thirty minutes every day and slowly work your way up to an hour or two, as you move into the more complex exercises of later chapters. With this type of practice, the actor begins to build a workable technique.

How an actor puts these simple tasks together will be unique to that individual. The resolution of the search for tension and its release will constitute the moment-to-moment technique so important to film acting. Eventually, the technique becomes second nature, and those that accomplish a smooth, even, gliding effect of moving, seemingly effortlessly from one moment to the next, will appear to be *just being themselves* and not acting at all, when, in fact, the ease with which they veil the mastering of technique is a tribute to their artistry.

CONCENTRATION

Let's suppose you've been sitting in the chair for about half an hour doing the Mental Relaxation exercises, and you find that your preoccupation with yourself is becoming unbearable. Perhaps it's time to concentrate on something else. Most actors will immediately want to escape to a character; they want to start acting. But there are a few steps that should take place before you start adding the distractions of a fictional being. In fact, it's much better to allow the self full reign, with just a gentle guiding hand and within a tighter sphere of concentration.

Concentration and observation are entwined with one another. In order to concentrate, you need something to focus on. In order to focus on something, you must have observed it first. You have to be aware that something exists, see it, notice it, discover it, investigate it, wonder about it, and care about it enough to focus and turn your concentration on it. What one chooses to focus on, what one chooses to concentrate on, comprises the elements that will make up the playing of a character or part.

Playing a character requires a series of complex choices in any medium, so it's best to start by investigating the raw material of you and discovering your responses to stimuli. In film acting, once a choice has been made, it must be executed successfully while the camera is rolling, and it must incorporate the moments of surprising discovery that will bring the character to life. The well-thought-out gestures of the theater may appear too large for the screen. They may appear too stagy or rehearsed for the critical eye of the camera, and therefore, not honest. The film audience wants to witness the moments of amazing clarity and brutal honesty that this medium can offer, a private viewing of a slice of life. It may be an extraordinary, unrealistic life, but with a performance that rings true to our human instincts. The continuous performance aspect of theater (starting a performance at the beginning and performing uninterrupted until the end) warrants a certain type of shaping and thought that is not necessary in film. The camera and the director will do the shaping. Also, the difference in distance from which the actor is viewed in the two mediums, so intensely close and personal in film and at varying degrees of distance depending on the performance space in theater, causes the film actor to be much more concerned with only the moment at hand. The committed theater actor may experience difficulty when adjusting to this concept and lack of control. In film, most of the time, actors are only required to bring truth to their gesture, and for the camera, the gesture must be like a laser: light, small, and extremely powerful.

The gesture originates from acute observation, but one cannot observe everything all at once all the time. A selection must be made. The selection, or choice, becomes the structure in which the focus can direct itself and concentration can begin to take place. The concentration of the actor should be weightless, accessible, easily carried anywhere, and simple to direct towards anything. Yet, this is rarely our impression of concentration, which usually conjures up ideas of heaviness, difficulty, and stillness. If we want to improve our concentration skills, I think it's best to start by observing how we concentrate.

OBSERVATION

In my acting classes, I try to make the students aware of how much their behavior can be affected by what their preconceived notions are of a word. If I tell them to really *concentrate* on their breathing, for example, to close their eyes and just concentrate on the breath, they will assume what they believe is the correct body posture and demeanor to indicate a state of intense concentration. Since they all know that they are in an acting class, the indications will be larger and more exaggerated than one might expect. Why this is, I'm not quite sure, but I think it's because most people think of acting as over-exaggerated expressions, very large. Someone has told them to do it that way, so that the audience can really get it in the back row, the "Sing out, Louise" school of acting, which, of course, is totally unnecessary for film.

It is amazing how quickly young actors can transform into old people. In order to carry out the simple task of concentration, almost all of them furrow their foreheads deeply, knit their eyebrows together, and clench their jaws. Their chins invariably get thrust in the air, and strangely enough, very often, their breathing stops for long periods of time and then becomes labored and unnatural. Breathing, which we do all day long, mostly without effort, becomes very difficult to do when we focus all our attention on it, particularly if we are in public, as we are in a class. What is innately easy and second nature becomes difficult. Instead of releasing the tension and allowing the natural flow of things to take place, one tries too hard. One tries either to force it into submission with muscle and will or becomes too passive and blank. Either way is demonstrated by a display of muscular tension, which does not make the situation any easier, nor does it alleviate the problem; it only complicates it. For an actor to succeed in observing either tendency in oneself is the first step in developing the concentration needed for the realm of "public privacy."

THE OBSERVATION EXERCISE

In my classes at the School of Visual Arts in New York City, I'm usually teaching first-year film and animation students a required course in acting. What this generally means is that they don't want to be in front of the camera, but in some capacity behind it. They come with the notion that acting is just something that certain types of people do well, and they are not aware that there is any technique or process involved. In my professional workshops, I often encounter people who want to be actors, driven by an inner desire that they have not yet discovered how to unleash, and they, too, are often burdened by the same misconceptions of acting. They experience fear and frustration because they haven't found the information they need to unlock their talents. I have tried to devise ways that will be easily accessible to anyone to help them discover the necessary techniques involved in the process. Since I believe that observation is key to understanding concentration, I start them off with the following simple exercise as their first assignment. It seems to work very well.

PUBLIC PRIVACY

This exercise asks you to do what you do for many hours every day, but within a preset amount of time and with keenly focused observation.

We spend many hours of each day walking or driving from one place to another, shopping or eating out somewhere, in an office or classroom, in an infinite number of places where we come in contact with other people. Many of them are strangers. Our thoughts drift from what we ourselves are doing to a streaming internal commentary on everything around us. We do this shift in thought unconsciously. Now, the idea is to do it consciously.

To frame this exercise, I use a quote of Konstantin Stanislavsky's from the book *Stanislavsky on the Art of the Stage*, translated by David Magarshack. This is my favorite of the books by and about Stanislavsky, and I have a dog-eared copy that I have carried around with me for twenty years. Stanislavsky is talking about the stage, but for the purpose of many aspects of acting, the inner workings of the actor are the same. Particularly for young actors, the film set will be their stage, and the rectangular of the frame is like that of the stage. It's still humans moving within a space; the outward space is different, but the inner space is the same.

Here's the quote:

> One must never think of the theatre as a place for some special sect of dedicated people. One must never look upon it as a place which is divorced from life. All the roads of creative human endeavor lead to a manifestation of life as "all roads lead to Rome." And the Rome of every man is one and the same; every man carries his entire creative genius within him, and he pours everything out of himself into the broad stream of life.

To focus one's concentration on the concept that "every man carries his entire creative genius within him, and he pours everything out of himself into the broad stream of life" is very important while doing this exercise. If we can suppose that everyone is worth observing, that through observing the world around us, we may find the way to observing ourselves, then the path to concentration becomes accessible and right in front of us, so to speak.

1 Choose a public place where you can sit undisturbed for a long period of time—a café, coffee shop, bar, park, etc., anywhere there are likely to be many people. It's best to choose a place where you are not likely to run into people whom you know, only because this is an exercise that you must do alone, without familiar company.

2 Bring a notebook for writing with you, which we'll call your Journal. The Journal becomes an important tool in this and in many other exercises, because it is easy to forget or reshape after the fact ideas, impressions, and feelings that happen spontaneously. It's best to write things down uncensored as they happen, and then read and think about them later.

3 Once you've settled down in your chosen place, set your watch for one hour. Time is such a strange thing, and our judgment of it depends on how we feel about what we're doing. Hours can fly

by unnoticed, and minutes can seem like hours, so check the clock and stay with it for one hour.

4 Observe the people around you, and write your observations in your Journal. Watch, observe, muse, and write. This is not continuous writing. Most of the time is spent observing.

5 While you are observing others, observe yourself and how you honestly feel at the moment. Start to write down these self-observations in your Journal as well. Be honest, stay in the moment. Try not to censor yourself.

6 Start by writing about what you see around you, or, if you are unable to do that, then write about how you feel about doing the exercise, then move it to the observations. Write about the people— who you think they are, where they come from, what they're doing, etc., or whatever aspects about them interest you. While you are doing this, try to see the creative genius in each person. Don't forget to include yourself.

NOTE ABOUT THE EXERCISE: You never know how you are going to react to a given situation in a given moment. Try to stay away from prejudgments and old ways of seeing things. Reread the Stanislavsky quote, and try to incorporate its message into your process. Encounter your preconception head on, and include your process of discovery about yourself and your surroundings in your Journal.

Remember! This is not a writing exercise, it's an observation exercise! It's an exercise of forcing yourself to concentrate on simple truths for one hour. The idea is to write what you are actually thinking. This is much more difficult than you might imagine. Grammar and spelling are not important; neither is complete sentence structure. The only thing that matters is that you write what's on your mind in the moment-to-moment reality.

7 When your hour is up, close your Journal and go about your life. Don't read what you've written just yet. Wait.

After at least a few hours, pick up your Journal and read it. You should try and be in some surrounding that will enable you to concentrate on your words and read them aloud without causing a problem. Try some of the Mental Relaxation exercises before you begin to read the Journal so you'll be in touch with yourself a little more.

As you read, ask yourself some of the following questions:

- Was I honest, and if I was, how do I feel about it now?

- When I started to feel something, what did I do? Did I investigate the feeling further, or did I quickly move on to something else?

- If someone seemed to notice what I was doing, how did I react?

- Did I go as far as I could have with my observations of my surroundings?

- Was I able to concentrate on the task at hand, or did I "drift" and then find myself lost in my thoughts?

- If and when I did this, did I admit it in writing, or was this self-observation omitted?

- Did I leave myself and my innermost feelings and observations totally out of this exercise? Why did I do that?

- Do I judge people so harshly that I tend to stereotype them, and if that's true, how would I portray them as an actor?

The answers to the above questions are not important. There is no right or wrong answer; there is only the development of a better question and the strengthening of your ability to ask. The process of developing observation and concentration is like working a muscle; it gets stronger with use. You have set parameters around your concentration by doing this exercise. Within these parameters, you can gauge your own performance and development. Each time you do an exercise, you can go a little bit further into the relaxation and concentration process.

ASSESSING THE EXERCISE

Now, look at your experience of the exercise. Did you suffer from self-consciousness? Could you see yourself trying to take that sense of self-consciousness and change it to self-discovery, which would lead you to deepening your observation and thereby your concentration?

The Observation exercise is useful to acting, because it places you in a public place doing an activity. Film actors never work separated by the stage from their audience. Film actors are always surrounded by people. On a low-budget film, it may only be a few people, but on a big-budget film, it could be hundreds. Therefore, the concentration must be developed publicly. They are watching you, but not for their own enjoyment. They, too, are working, and *their* concentration is totally pinned on you while the camera is rolling. The actors' close proximity to those around them requires a sense of a circle of concentration that is focused and strong, yet relaxed and easy. To sit in a public place while you know you have an agenda enables you to slowly start to become aware of what stops you from simply observing yourself and your surroundings. Also, the act of self-discovery, so exciting to see on the screen, begins to emerge in this simple exercise.

Can you observe when your ability to concentrate wavers and what impedes it? Are you willing to whittle away at the things that stand in your way? I always say it's like being a sculptor. When Michelangelo ordered the marble for the *Pietà* and it arrived, did he say, "Oh no, that's too huge a mass of rock. I'll never be able to do anything with that!" Well, maybe he did in his mind, but in his studio, he took out his hammer and chisel and began work. He chipped away little piece by little piece, until he was able to liberate the forms from within the solid mass. Actors are like that huge, rough rock of marble, and our hammer and chisel is the focus of our concentration. Little chip by little chip, we liberate the raw stuff of expression within ourselves, which later becomes the characters we play. The communication of this inner expression is realized through concentration, along with the moment-to-moment relaxation process and the use of the senses.

SENSE MEMORY

We observe the world through our senses. We have five (and the much-talked-about sixth sense, which is another matter altogether). Our five senses bring us through the world each day, translating everything that we experience into a language that we understand. Then, through our senses, we are able to communicate back to the world around us.

Our senses have a memory, a ship's log, of everything we've experienced, encapsulated somewhere within. To become aware of the power of that memory and its use in acting is a lifelong pursuit. There are volumes written about sense memory, what it is, and how it should be taught and used. The teachings of Lee Strasberg and Stanislavsky are hotly debated and discussed; I am not going to get embroiled in that here. Certainly, one needs an excellent teacher to learn the complexities of sense memory, but there is a lot that can be done on one's own to develop and strengthen the use of the senses. If the work appeals to you, you can always start to look for a teacher to take you further down the path.

First, let's take a brief look at each sense and how we experience it in our memory. In later chapters, I'll go into each of the senses and how the sensorial memory can be used in film acting.

SIGHT: THE SENSE OF SEEING

We see through our eyes and also very strongly in our mind's eye. If you close your eyes, the act of seeing often continues, with memories, colors, and dreams. Sitting in a chair as in the Mental Relaxation exercise, with your eyes closed, think of different things you know well, which come up spontaneously, and allow the eyes to wander through different places. This will be much like the beginning of the first chapter, where we went through our favorite movie scenes.

Now, take your bedroom at home. This "home bedroom" will mean different things to different people; it may be a place in the present, or it may be one of the past. It doesn't matter which one it is. The first room that comes into view in your mind's eye is the right one to use now.

How much of it can you *see*? If you look at the walls, can you see the pictures on them or the color of the paint or wallpaper? Ask yourself how much better your vision becomes if you focus your concentration onto a specific point or aspect by posing a question. Example: If I turn my mind's eye to the left wall of my room, what is there? (Obviously, you know what's there because it's your room, but turn your focus to the wall anyway, and see what your inner concentration shows you.)

Don't assume you know the answer; allow the vision to reveal to you how much you know. This is key to developing the concentration and the senses. You may be very surprised by what happens when you pose a question and wait to discover the answer. Continue the process with the rest of the room, posing a question, waiting for the answer through what you *see*. Keep your eyes closed; keep the concentration on the eyes and the process of seeing.

SOUND: THE SENSE OF HEARING

Hearing is accomplished by the ears, but unlike sight and our eyes, which we deal with in a more conscious way, hearing and the ears are taken greatly for granted by many people. Unless one is gifted or a trained musician, hearing is done unconsciously most of the time. So, let's consider the ear and its construction. Try and feel the ear canal and the outer part of the ear, which "catches" the sound. Now, place yourself in the same bedroom at home, still with your eyes closed (it's easier to concentrate that way, we'll open them later), and try and hear the sounds of that room. Again, pose questions:

Am I alone in the house? If not, do I hear anyone else? If I look out the window, what do I hear? Does the room have sounds of its own? The water in the pipes, sounds of wind, the window blinds tapping slightly against the wall? If I concentrate on my ears, what do I hear?

Listen to the sounds; feel them in your ears. If your body is relaxed, it will react to the sounds that you hear.

SMELL: THE SENSE OF SMELLING

We smell things with our nose and the inside of its membranes. The sense of smell has been attributed to have the most powerful emotional recall capacities. I don't know if that's really true, but from my own experience, I have often found it to be.

In the same room, your bedroom, with your eyes closed, take in a deep breath with all your focus on your sense of smell. As the air comes through your nose, pose the questions: What do I smell? Is there a linden tree blooming outside my window or someone cooking in another room? The lingering scent of someone's perfume? A distinct smell, which I can't identify, but that I associate with this place?

Whatever you come up with, you might get flooded by the other senses. Memories or scenarios might appear that charge the concentration with data. Don't worry about these things now, and don't get sidetracked by them. Stay within the chosen task by asking questions. Acknowledge whatever goes on in your mind, and move forward with the concentration on the sense that you are working on.

TASTE: THE SENSE OF TASTING

Ahhh! The mouth, tongue, and lips. What a trio! If you take some time out and consider all the functions of this triumvirate while moving your tongue over your lips and within the inside of your mouth, many interesting things may start to happen. Spend some time with this and explore.

The first sensorial taste to introduce should be lemon. It's a strong taste and causes many reactions within the mouth. Lick the tongue over the lips as if you had just sucked on a juicy lemon. Swallow; investigate the roof of the mouth. Ask questions: What happens to my lips if I taste a lemon? How does my tongue feel? Where do I taste the taste of lemon?

Don't worry if nothing happens. If you don't taste the lemon, or for that matter don't respond to any of the senses in your imagination at this point, remember these are concentration exercises. We are not working for results; we're just doing inventory. We are moving through our repertoire of stimuli to discover what creates a strong reaction and formulating the necessary structure from which to work our concentration.

Try combining the senses of smell and taste. Think of one of your favorite foods as a child, something associated with where you come from. Now, try to smell its aroma. Even if it's ice cream, it has a smell. Move from the scent to the taste by moving the sensation around the mouth, tongue, and lips.

TOUCH: THE SENSE OF FEELING

Touch is an enormous field of experience. The skin, which we are encased in, is the obvious emperor of this sense, but the entire inner organism also experiences feelings, feelings like muscle ache, tickles, indigestion, and heartbeats. At this time, we'll only be dealing with the skin and, more expressly, the hands. If we stop and think of all the things our hands do, all of the millions of things they have touched and experienced, we will quickly see how vast their work for us has been.

Let's go back to the same "home bedroom." You are still sitting in a chair with your eyes closed. Extend one of your hands out into the space before you, and imagine that you are touching the covering of your bed. Don't know beforehand what it will feel like—that is to say, "Oh, now, I'm going to touch that soft, flannel bedspread." Just let the hand reach into space, and in the mind's eye, see it gently "touching" the covering on the bed. Then, pose the questions: Where do I feel it on my hand? If I move my hand back and forth lightly, can I feel the texture of the fabric? Am I breathing steadily and fully? If I take a deep breath and relax my shoulders, can I get more sensation from my hand?

Explore the sensation. Bring in the other hand to touch the bed covering. Don't let the fingers bunch together. Always leave a space between you and your imagination.

THE PROCESS OF RELAXATION, CONCENTRATION, AND SENSE MEMORY

Many actors begin to work on characters by asking a lot of questions. What should I do? How should I play this? What's my activity, my action? And so on. All are valid questions, which they will try and answer intellectually and then create behavior that indicates the sum of their answers. However, they have predetermined how the character will act, and this can appear too artificial. Particularly in the case of stage actors, the resulting gestures are often too broad for the camera and the film medium.

However, for many actors, not knowing the answers to all the questions right away creates a lot of physical and mental tension that blocks their ability to focus the concentration on the more unique aspects of the character. If they were to learn to trust the sense memory, many of the answers they seek would be found, but in an ever-evolving form, brought about by the process of relaxation, concentration, and sense memory.

Film acting is usually quite small and subtle. There's a gentleness to it that is magnified by the camera. The smallest thought, or change in expression of the eyes, is captured. The actor is often confined to an uncomfortable space during a shot, and a particular scene might be filmed dozens of times in different angles and takes, with the actor repeating essentially the same things over and over again. Often, there is little space in which the actor can move. Each time must appear fresh and real. Theatrical gestures and many choices that one can use on the stage will not do under these circumstances. A smaller gesture, with its origins organically stemming from the actor, is required for this environment.

So, what starts happening when you stop doing these broader gestures and are only left with yourself? At first, it feels like nothing. Nothing is happening. It feels like there is a void. In actuality, that void is the open, fertile, planting fields of your imagination. Here, you drop the sacred seeds of your chosen concentration. It is very difficult to adjust to doing this. It takes courage to reach the point of relaxation wherein you can observe what you must stop doing and allow the space to open up inside, for the unknown possibilities of what at first feels like nothing. This is the beginning of concentration and the acceptance of the fact that you yourself are more than enough to play the part. The void is often associated with the dark, with uncertainty and not knowing what to do next. For a film actor, this is the perfect place to be. This is the beginning of the search. The chosen concentration in the form of sensorial memory is projected into this space like a laser. From this thin ray of light, something organic begins to develop and take over the whole being. It is from this resource that impulses will arise and the development of a character ready to go before the cameras starts to emerge.

This character must be a talking, breathing human being (well, most of the time anyway). It's time to open our eyes, to start thinking about how the breath and the voice and the text come into this process and affect the relaxation, concentration, and the playing of a part.

THE VOICE AND THE BREATH

Throughout the previous two chapters, I have repeatedly reminded you to remember to breathe. Each new step in the process of relaxation and concentration must be accompanied by checking the breath in order to investigate the moment fully. It is in the simple process of sufficient breathing, so that the emotion of the moment can move freely through you, that you discover what the moment is all about. Through the breath, we discover what we are experiencing in our entire selves. Just try it yourself. Take one of the sense memories that you used from the previous chapter, and each time you discover a sensation or memory, concentrate on the breath. I think you will find that the breath opens up the experience and makes it more alive.

It is not by chance that it is said that actors breathe life into their parts. Actors take the written part and give it a breath, a voice, and a soul. When actors read parts, they see them in their minds. They have impressions and ideas that flesh out the scenario and make it come to life. The imagination of the actor takes away special nuggets from this reading process, which it will use to begin the creation of the character whom the actor will eventually play. One of the essential elements of this process is the actor's own breath, the life-sustaining flow of air that accompanies every moment of our lives and must also flow through the life of the character.

As you deepen your relaxation and direct your concentration to tighter and more refined circles of focus, this breath, which gives way to making sounds and eventually the voice, is the beginning of the recognition of the impulses that are being released from within. You must continually remind yourself to breathe, especially when you are beginning work on a character. Many questions arise that need to be answered, and it's easy to forget that breathing is part of the process.

Proper breathing is an obvious fundamental of any acting technique, but what I'm talking about is how the moment-to-moment reality is dependent upon the free and easy breath being appropriate to the emotion of the moment. In film acting, since it isn't necessary to project the voice, the breathing and vocal patterns should be more as they are in everyday life. They aren't consistent; they are surprising, and they often catch you off guard. This is one of the essential differences between film and theater acting. In film, the breath and the voice can be more consistent with the details of the moment, rather than being a set of preplanned directions dictated by the demands of the play and the performance space. The film actor is asked to deliver the details of the moment as realistically as possible: a secret whispered and shared in the dark, intimate words that get stuck in your throat, screams and cries that would throw a stage actor out of the show for a week because of voice damage, long periods of intense listening that are photographed in close-up. All these moments must be filled with the subtle nuances of your own unique personality; they are rarely filled by words. The camera has the power to perceive the smallest nuances, ones so subtle that they would never read on stage, but when they are photographed, these nuances become radiant. It is the breath that carries the nuance to the screen and communicates its meaning to the audience.

For the actor on the stage, vocal production and projection take precedence over the emotional moment when speaking. For the actor on film, the emotional moment and its nuances take precedence.

However, even in film, when the pressures of performing create an intense atmosphere for the actor, the breath (and the voice) can become stilted and too controlled. When this happens, the actor must go back to the relaxation checking process, focusing the concentration and breathing into the moment. This happens to the experienced professional as well as the beginner. Wherever you are in the spectrum of acting experience, training, and technique, the approaches to managing the problems of shallow breath and stilted speech are the same. From the very beginning, work on these problems should be integrated into the work on yourself and the character.

To explore the process of how the breath and voice are integrated into a character, we should first choose a character to work on as a basis for doing the exercises. This is a discovery process, a discovery of yourself and you as the character.

CHOOSING THE RIGHT PRACTICE MATERIAL

When choosing a part to work on with the intention of using it as a basis to expand your knowledge of either a technique or of your talent, it is best to follow some important rules.

1 The part must be of your sex and appropriate age range. "Age range" is a professional acting term used to describe the range of ages that you are able to play at any given time in your life. Age

range is extremely important in the film world. Since the camera comes in very close to photograph your face, you must look believably like the age that you are playing. The age range usually runs in five- to ten-year spans around your real age. For instance, if you are thirty years old, then your age range runs approximately from twenty-five to thirty-five years old. Sometimes, the age range is less than ten years, depending on the person. It is rarely more. This doesn't mean that you will never play a part outside of your age range, but for our purposes now, we will stay within it.

2 Choose a part from a well-known, successful play or movie. It's best to take a part from the beginning of the piece to work on. Don't choose a piece that has been written by you or a friend of yours. Also, make sure it's dramatic text. No poetry, transcripts from novels, excerpts from diaries, etc. If possible, start at the beginning, when the character is first introduced. You should avoid the climaxes and final speeches for now.

3 The character should be saying something that you find interesting, something that is important to you. It's best if you feel passionate about it.

4 It should be a block of text of at least ten or fifteen lines that is completely uninterrupted by another character talking. If another character's text is interspersed with yours, the monologue should still make sense if those lines are omitted.

5 The character's experience in life should to some degree parallel your own. In other words, the character should be struggling with issues that you understand because of your own experience and knowledge. The best situation is when you understand what the struggle is, but have yet to come up with a resolution on your own. Perhaps, then, you and the character can discover something together. It also helps if you and the character come from the same economic background.

6 Avoid high or physical comedy, period pieces with difficult text, parodies, or surrealistic material. These forms require more complicated approaches to be acted properly. Don't use sitcom material. This doesn't mean that the piece can't have a sense of humor or be complex, but it's best to stick to fairly contemporary works whose characters are people you feel you know.

7 If you are a beginner in acting or someone who has acting experience but just hasn't gotten film work, then avoid any part with an accent other than your own.

In other words, try and choose a part that is as close to you as possible. If you have difficulty doing this or are unfamiliar with the repertoire out there, ask someone to recommend roles to you. Even the know-it-all guy who works in your local video store or theater bookstore may be able to help more than you might realize. People who love film and theater are usually more than willing to share what they know if they are asked.

Once you have chosen the part that you want to work on, read through the entire script once or twice, and then put it away. Choose the segment that you are going to work on, and write or type out the monologue on a piece of paper. Don't even worry about memorizing it.

THE FIRST STEPS TO GIVING THE CHARACTER YOUR VOICE

What we are going to do now is to start to incorporate a fictional character into the relaxation and concentration process. One way of doing this is to read some of the words that the character speaks, but only as you, without trying to impose characteristics on them. You should always start with what you can do easily and avoid (at least for now) searching away from yourself, making things more complicated. Reading words from a piece of paper is an easy thing to do if you are just being you and not worrying about playing a part. The work on the character comes later.

Take your piece of paper with the words on it and your Journal, and go to a place where you will be able to work. This place should be somewhere where you could make noise if necessary. Do a physical warm-up if you know one. If you don't, stretching, jogging, or jumping in place are all good things to do to get the blood flowing and the breath connected to the body.

Once your breath is moving freely through your body, sit comfortably and do the Mental Relaxation Exercises. Take your time here. If you have just read the script, the character you have chosen will already be working within you, though you might not be consciously aware of it. I have often heard people say, "You work on it, and it works on you." We generally have much more information in ourselves than we need to play the part, so just try and stay in the present moment and investigate it fully by using the system of the Mental Relaxation. If you stay in the present moment, it will lead to the next moment and the discoveries needed to play the part.

Here are some things that you should be aware of while you sit doing the Mental Relaxation:

- Place all your concentration on your breathing. Allow the thoughts, images, and feelings to flow through your breath freely and easily. Sometimes, the idea of blowing an image up like a balloon or keeping a feeling alive, as if it were a feather afloat in the air, helps to keep the breath connected to the moment.

- If the breath gets caught or you feel yourself spacing out, sigh. Sighing is done by bringing the air high into the chest, then letting it all out at once. It releases tension and uncovers things you didn't know were there. Ask yourself, "When do I sigh in life?" It's often when you have feelings that you can't express. Sighing is often a flag signifying that emotions need to be expressed.

- Don't sit on the breath by allowing it to fall down into the navel area; keep the breath moving in the upper chest. Emotions are most easily expressed and released when the breath is high in the body. Just watch an excited or upset child's breathing or a very angry person's breath pattern, and you will see how the chest moves as if the emotion were riding on it.

- When you feel yourself getting distracted, feel a strong sensation, or can identify an impulse happening anywhere in the body, make a long continuous AHHH sound. The throat should be open, and the sound should waver with the changes that you experience while you are making it. This sound can be soft, or it can be very loud; it depends on the moment.

- Direct your concentration back and forth between the relaxation process, breathing, sighing, and making sounds.

After about fifteen or twenty minutes of Mental Relaxation, pick up your piece of paper with your monologue on it, and read the first line. You know, I always find that the nice thing about a piece of paper with words on it is that it doesn't change. It is a concrete object that can be moved, carried, crumpled, and thrown; it will still have the same words written on it. You don't have to be worried about destroying it, and you shouldn't be afraid of it. If you have problems saying any of the text, the problems can be fixed later. Speech and pronunciation are different steps in the process of acting; in fact, they are separate studies all together, studies that have easily accessible answers. The words are simply there; they won't suddenly change or shift like you might. You can worry about memorizing them later. You are the changing force; you are the thing that brings about the metamorphosis of the words into the character. The words only give voice to your changes, and your breath gives them their meaning by the way that you say them.

So please, don't read even the first line with a preordained expression that has no connection with how you really feel in the moment. Just read the words on the page as though they had nothing to do with the script and everything to do with your immediate state. If you have thought too much about the part and how you think it should be played, this will not be an easy thing to do. You have already created a preconceived notion of how you should sound. Your mind has worked too quickly, and you have already made decisions, which will condemn your character to a narrower sphere of existence than is necessary. You have already gotten "stuck in your head."

GETTING STUCK IN YOUR HEAD

When you stop being in the moment—that is, stop experiencing the entire body and all the senses in this very instance of time—and start thinking about what is happening instead of feeling it, the moment cannot be properly investigated. You have allowed the process to leave the physical body and go into the mind. This is often referred to as being stuck, or being in your head, or the worst state—being stuck in your head.

One of the biggest problems with being stuck in your head is that you are not aware of it, or if you are aware of it, you don't think that it's a problem. It seems normal, which it is for many circumstances; it's just not good for this circumstance. So, you need some way of recognizing that it has happened. Then, you can extricate yourself and move on.

Being stuck is often signaled by a near stoppage or shallowing of the breath. If your concentration is tipped towards checking your breathing, then you will be able to get back to the body, the experience, and breathing fully into the investigation of the next moment.

THE PRECONCEIVED IDEA

When my students are presenting a monologue for the first time, they always want to memorize all the words, come in gangbusters, and present a complete character ready for the camera. They aren't able to do this on the first try. They panic and freeze, because they don't know what to do to begin simply. I always tell them, "Don't worry, the Academy Awards aren't for another six weeks, and you weren't even nominated this year, so we have plenty of time to explore. Just relax and start breathing. Just look at us and breathe." They experience tension and anxiety because of their own expectations. All I want them to do is to look at us, breathe into the moment, and read the first lines. That's where they should begin.

The unconscious workings of an actor's talent are a vast field of contradictions. No one knows how it really works, but one can safely say that it works differently for everybody. One thing is probably true of everybody though: The things we want the most are most difficult for us to do. If you are up against an extreme desire to do well as an actor, and almost certainly you are (it tends to come with the territory), then you will experience the pressure to succeed. The desire to measure up to your own expectations will be very strong.

In the world of film, with its idols and enormous faces confronting us in the dark, the expectations that you have to measure up to these images can be very daunting. They take on the role of a god or idol, and you will always fall short of your own expectations. It is often the case that in the initial work on a character, these expectations will arise and impose themselves on your work. Your voice will not be connected to the present moment, because you are not connected to it. You are thinking about something in the past (your first impression of the character) and how you want it to affect the results of the future (your performance of the part). It is not the present moment.

When this happens, you have formed a preconceived idea about how the character should be played, and this will get in the way of your discovery process. A preconceived idea will cause you to get stuck in your head. These ideas start to enforce themselves upon your behavior. You find that you are dictating the moments to yourself to comply with your preconceived idea. It is possible to stop this from happening by simply concentrating on the breath and going back to the body and your own organic reality of the moment. The breath will breathe life into the moment, and you will start the process of discovering the parts of you that the character has inspired.

Very seasoned professionals can create characters that they have played in various incarnations almost instantaneously. Comedians do this all the time. They have done their groundwork, and now, they are just delivering the goods. Students and actors who are trying to expand their instruments have to go back to the discovery process. Even seasoned professionals, if they are worth their salt, continue the discovery process instinctively at every chance. They have learned through experience how much more exciting their work is when they do this.

THE INNER MONOLOGUE WITH TEXT

Let's go back to sitting in the chair. You have just read the first line of the monologue. If you find that your preconceived ideas about the character are already at work, then just stop, take a deep breath, and try to do the following:

1 Believe that your inspiration will make sense of all the things that you are trying to do, and just stay in the moment. You must trust yourself. Don't try to answer all your questions at once. Remember, at this point, it's not about right and wrong, it's just about doing and investigating.

2 Check the eyes and the back of the head for rising tension, and release this tension by sighing or making the AHHH sound.

3 Speak your thoughts aloud as in the Inner Monologue. Place all judgments of your performance of these exercises on the character. In other words, if you are very critical of yourself, then the character has a critical nature. If you feel too big and strong for this moment sitting in this chair, then it is the character who has these feelings about her environment. Whatever your thoughts, speak them out loud.

4 If you find yourself getting stuck in your head, try Gibberish.

5 Make loud AHHH sounds to release the buildup of mental and physical tension.

6 If you feel nothing is happening, then do the same thing you did in step #3: Put the way that you feel on the character, and make very loud AHHH sounds. Speak your thoughts out loud.

7 Occasionally, look down at the text and say whatever line your eyes see. Don't be concerned with order; the page has the order, and it will be there for you later. Allow your inner instrument to use your breath and your voice without your interference.

8 Keep going back to checking the breath. Make sure you are getting enough air.

9 If you are a trained stage actor or a singer, try not to fill your chest with air and support before you speak. Speak softly, so you don't need as much support. Be diligent about checking for tension in the upper body region.

10 Go back and forth between the Mental Relaxation, breathing, sighing, the text, Gibberish, and the Inner Monologue, until the text is just another part of the discovery process, no more or no less important than the other things that you are doing. Give your own words the same power as the words of the character. Keep moving forward into the next moment.

11 If you feel the need to get up, move around, or lie on the floor while you are doing these things, please feel free to do so, but stay in the chair for at least twenty minutes before getting up. If you get up and move around too quickly, you can miss some of the more subtle impulses that are very useful to this process.

12 After at least forty-five minutes, pick up your Journal and write. Write whatever you like. It's best if you can write an assessment of the exercise, adding your thoughts about the character as you go along. You can also include any revelations you have had about yourself. However, many times you'll want to write about something that seems, at the time, totally unrelated to the exercise you have just completed. Don't worry about it, just go ahead and write whatever comes to you first. There's usually important information there that you will be able to use later on.

THE JOURNAL AS INNER VOICE

The Journal is a useful tool for actors. It gives them an added space to work in that is very private. It is where they can assess what they have just done immediately after they have done it.

When you write in your Journal right after an exercise, you have a way of remembering everything for later. Often when you are working, the impressions have been so plentiful that it is difficult to remember them all. It is also true that something that made no sense to you at the moment becomes clearer with time, or vice versa. The Journal takes the burden off of the memory, which allows the actor to relax more thoroughly. It serves as an inner private voice. What you write after an exercise will often reveal surprising results. It unlocks the creativity in a different way, expressing many things that were there lying below the surface, unable to emerge. The

Journal has given you the opportunity to voice these things privately. You have just given reign to many impulses and images, much information has passed through you, and now, you need to make a record of it that you can go back to later.

Sometimes, the writings will say things that would be difficult for you to say out loud, even if no one else were around. It is the expression of this inner voice that the actor needs to be thinking of while he or she is saying the text of a character.

ASSESSING THE EXERCISE IN YOUR JOURNAL

Each person develops his or her own style of Journal writing. Since it is a private space, it must make sense only to you. I teach a lot of artists and animators acting, and they often cover their books with scribbling and drawings. It works for them; no one else has to understand it. As in the Observation Exercise, the Journal work is not a literary exercise. The sentences don't have to be complete; spelling and grammar are not important. What is important is the information that you are saving for yourself.

There should be a system of question asking and answering that you set up for yourself. Ask and answer some of the following questions:

- Was I able to be aware of getting stuck in my head? If I was aware of it, how did I change it?

- Was I aware of my preconceived ideas and how they got in my way? What did I do to change my behavior, and where did it lead me?

- Could I just stop what I was doing and breathe into the moment? What happened when I did this?

- How did the breath change the moment?

- Did I learn something I didn't know about the character by allowing it to live through me? What was it?

- Did the text continually come out the same way even though I tried to change it? Why do I think I had this difficulty?

- Am I satisfied with my work, or am I dissatisfied because I am pressured by an idea of performing for an audience in the future?

- Was I able to stay in the moment? When I was in the moment, what did it feel like?

- What is the next thing I would like to accomplish for this character?

- Was I speaking in my own voice, or did my voice sound foreign to me?

- Did I find myself avoiding certain lines or passages in the text? Why do I think that was?

- Did I hurt my throat by speaking or yelling too loudly, or was it difficult to get the sound out at all? What were the emotions connected to these moments?

There are many questions that you can ask and answer. These are just examples. One should develop a habit of questioning and seeking answers in all acting work. The Journal is like a map that you are charting. You are wandering through new territory, and you will need more than bread crumbs to find your way back again. It charts your path. It reminds you of where you have been and helps you find out where you want to go.

THE TRAINED VOICE

Actors and singers with trained voices encounter different problems when trying to adjust to film acting. Their instruments have been disciplined for projection, power, and stamina. The muscles that create a trained voice are strong and ready to support them when performing. These muscles affect the stance of the whole body and are often not willing to disengage to allow the more natural speech that is needed for film. These muscles, when not used for projection, can create a great deal of tension for the performer new to the film medium. The performer feels like he isn't doing enough, because he no longer has to worry about the volume.

The best thing to do for this problem is to become aware of it. To be more conscious of the muscles engaging when you are speaking, choose a difficult classical monologue that you have memorized or performed. Lay down on the floor and breathe. Start your emotional preparation, and allow it to take a strong hold on your body. Do the monologue sotto voce, as if you were speaking to someone who was leaning over you, listening very closely to every word that you are saying. It should feel very intimate. Be aware of taking the time to be completely relaxed while speaking and breathing. Pay particular attention to your back and leg muscles. Don't worry about devoicing (a voice that is only half produced and close to whispering), especially when the emotion is powerful.

Try to relax all of your back muscles, and allow the breath to move high into the chest. Allow the emotion to take control. Break up the patterns by including the Inner Monologue and taking pauses for breathing. Work very slowly. Every time the muscles engage to project the voice out, try to relax them and lower your volume. Keep the jaw muscles slack. This may cause you to lose control of pronunciation, but don't worry about it for now. You'll be able to fix that later.

If you have a highly skilled vocal technique, then you have already set up a dialogue with your instrument. You should be able to adjust it to a more intimate context. After doing the monologue lying down, try it again, this time sitting up while still on the floor. Then, take it to a chair and so on, until you are standing up and moving around, while still maintaining the intimate nature of the speech. This exercise should set you on the road to finding a way to adjust your instrument for film.

VOLUME

The comment will often come up in my acting classes that the actors couldn't be heard while doing a monologue or scene. I always ask whether or not the observers believed the behavior of the actors. That's what I am watching for: Did I believe the actor's body language? Was his face expressive? Was it interesting to *watch*? The volume of the performance isn't important to me all the time. If I found that the behavior was truthful, that I believed that the actor was in the place or the situation that he was trying to portray, then I am not concerned about whether or not I can hear him. The voice at proper levels of sound can be fixed later, or even added in later, as is often the case on film productions. (Recording the voice after the film has been shot is called "looping." The actor stands in front of a very sensitive microphone wearing the headset that is attached to it. He watches his film performance, as he speaks the words in sync with his character's lips. This requires great listening skills.)

Devoicing isn't a problem in film acting for the most part. We often devoice in life when we are unsure of ourselves or when we are experiencing strong emotions like fear. Shyness, a quality fascinating to watch, often causes devoicing as well. Sometimes, it is a signal that the actor hasn't found an essential element for the character, so the voice will pull back or even stop all together. This happens to allow the actor to investigate what is missing and fill the moment with the nuances of her own discovery process.

One should never just plow through and force the voice to cover with volume what is missing from the inner life.

Eventually, even the film actor must bring up the volume slightly, so as not to hurt the voice, but it doesn't have to be a priority as it is in the theater. Once actors preparing for film work program this into their process, the process becomes much easier, and the instrument is free to relax and investigate more thoroughly.

On the stage, sound, including the actor's voice, signals the audience to direct their attention to that sound. In film, the audience watches what is on the screen before them. What they should pay attention to has been chosen for them by the camera frame. Many times, the one who is speaking is not the one who is in the frame. The one we are watching is the one who is listening, just as the audience is.

The essential elements of all acting are the same, but the process of preparing for a film role takes different steps and priorities than stage acting. Everything must start with the relaxation and the focus of the concentration. Then, the breath must move through each moment to investigate it fully. The voice expresses the moment in either sound or words. You should always start with your own words; the actual text comes last. To make this process work takes a lot of skill, and time must be invested.

The next four chapters are about using the senses to create different aspects of your character and performance in front of a camera. You always use the process of relaxation and concentration as your starting point.

We will start with listening. Within the intimate box of the camera frame, it is this skill that takes the place of the powerful stage voice. Listening to the other actors, listening to the world around you, and listening to your own inner voice.

LISTENING

Perhaps one of the most important abilities that all actors share is the great skill of listening. Actors are continually developing their ability to listen to each other and to listen to themselves while acting. It is one of the abilities that allows actors to take in what is happening around them. They hear, they react to what they hear, and they respond. Through their response, we gain knowledge of the world, both internal and external, in which they exist. The simplicity, and therein the profound difficulty of listening is often greatly underestimated by nonactors or beginners, but as an actor gains more and more experience, it becomes apparent how very important this skill is in the circle of acting concentration.

On the screen, the camera's close range invites us to see the actors engaged in an extremely refined form of listening. We share the private worlds of the characters in the story, and we see their reactions in a way that is reserved for only the most intimate of human relations in life. A large part of this intimacy is how we see the characters reacting to what is being said to them, as if we were there talking to them ourselves; we see them not only listening to others, but listening to their own inner thoughts. Listening to your own inner thoughts is often called thinking. When we witness the actor's thoughts on the screen, we are drawn into the story, and if it is a well-made movie, we identify with the characters and experience with them.

WATCHING MOVIE SCENES FOR LISTENING

The best way to show you how important listening is to film acting is to tell you to watch great movies while paying particular attention to how and when the actors listen, how what they hear causes them to act, and how they respond.

Casablanca is a great film to watch for the skill of listening. There are many examples of actors using their sense of hearing to tell the story in this film. Some of the strongest scenes are when the characters are simply listening to music. There are several in this film.

The first one occurs shortly after Ilsa's (Ingrid Bergman) entrance, when she asks Sam to play it once again. Here, we see the desire, and the reluctance, to hear the song, "As Time Goes By," which will evoke memories of a complicated past. The close-ups of Bergman humming and then listening to this song light up the screen in immortal images of love lost and desire. In wonderful contrast to Ilsa's radiant light, Rick (Humphrey Bogart) listens to the same song shortly thereafter in a dark scene of despair and drunkenness. His torture and conflict are apparent as we watch him simply sit at a table and listen to the song. The two scenes are constructed by the director and script in such a way that we are drawn into their world, present and past, simply by having watched them listen to the song that links their relationship to one another. The work of the actor appears very simple—sit and listen—but it is clear when you watch these scenes that this simple act must be performed to its fullest potential in order to achieve such a poignant effect.

LISTENING IN LIFE

When you are listening in acting, you are using one of your senses, your sense of hearing. Many times, you are actually listening to something that is there, like the sound of the other actor's voice. Many other times, you are listening from memory, because the actual sounds that the audience hears when the film is finished are not present when you are shooting. What you are doing is listening and reacting to sounds from your own creative memory.

In order to use this skill effectively in professional acting, it must be developed specifically for that purpose. The best way to start developing it is to become aware of what you listen to in your daily life and how it affects you.

If you ask most people what they listen to, they will name some sort of music or a radio station. They will not normally respond with something like, "Oh, I listen to the rain" or "I love to listen to the sound of the children's playground across the street" or "I listen to all the noise inside my head." In fact, we listen to all kinds of things all day long, and all of them affect our actions and decisions. Our hearing, like all our senses, works diligently to warn, protect, comfort, and inform us of the world around us. There are thousands of mundane sounds that we hear in our daily lives, and the situations that surround them constitutes what these sounds mean to us.

On Tuesday, September 11, 2001, the day of the terrorist attack on the World Trade Center, I was at home in my Manhattan apartment working on this very chapter. I had the radio on, and although I was not *listening* to it, I heard the announcement that Tower One of the World Trade Center had been hit by an airplane. I could not see the Towers from my windows, nor could I hear the first explosion and all the horrific sounds that followed, but every sound of that day is indelibly seared into my memory for the rest of my life.

I remember the sounds of the constant barrage of sirens coming from every direction, all heading furiously downtown. The sound of my husband's key in our apartment door, which filled me with a sense of relief: "Thank God, he's alive, he's safe." The sound of a family member's or friend's voice on the other end of the telephone: "Thank God, they are alive, they're safe." The sound of a phalanx of heavy construction vehicles going down Second Avenue in the early evening, their front-end loaders, cranes, digging, and towing apparatuses creaking as they moved determinedly towards what was by then already called Ground Zero.

The most chilling sound of that day was the sound of silence that night, a sound one never hears living in Manhattan. We live next to Bellevue Hospital, where hundreds of doctors and emergency workers stood waiting for the injured. I went to bed expecting the constant sound of the ambulance siren to prevail throughout the night and took that as an awaited comfort, trusting that the good doctors would do their jobs. I awoke two or three times that night in a sweat, panic and sorrow surrounding my chest like a death grip, to the sound of absolute silence. Silence, no ambulances, no sound, very few survivors, silence.

Those like myself, who were not at Ground Zero that day, will remember it through the mundane sounds of ordinary life—a key in the door, the sound of a voice, the roll of a tractor's motor. These sounds, and many others, took on extraordinary meaning on a day that will alter our lives for many years to come. A strange kind of clarity came over me that day. There was a stripping away of what was unimportant; I made choices in the moment as well as for the future. I separated what had meaning from what was essentially meaningless; the world was filled with a sense of immediacy. Every moment became precious, and within the catastrophe around me, I realized how precious life is. Life is a series of moments, perceptions, and choices, but above all, it is painfully short. Life should be lived to the fullest. The present moment is everything.

SETTING UP A SENSORY STRUCTURE

Sensorial choices in acting are not usually made from the remnants of such a historical day, but one can gauge from such a day what constitutes a powerful experience. Whenever you are making choices for acting, they should be made with the rich immediacy of things that are important to you. No one has to understand why a particular sensorial choice holds so much power for you; that is your own private matter. The choice must have power in order to fuel your character with a sense of urgency and reality. The script will tell the story. As an actor, you must supply the moments of life.

It is impossible to say what a great actor used to achieve a certain effect in a classic scene that has been immortalized by time. To do so is only speculation, but any actor working today can use his or her own senses and develop them for greater effect while acting. Actors can find their own way of putting it together and bringing it to the screen.

By saying "putting it together," I mean taking the results of the sensory exercises and using them in varying and uniquely personal ways, based on your investigation and assessment during the exercise. In order to do this, you have to set up a system of working that is consistent and disciplined. First, you observe yourself in your everyday life, and then, you set up a structure for disciplined work. One ought to work for two straight hours at least four times a week. The work should consist of the Relaxation exercises and then a sensory exercise. The sensory exercise may lead you into character work or may be done for the sole purpose of exploring your sensorial instrument's possibilities. The sensory work is always done very slowly at first, each moment being fully investigated and checked for truth and reality. It is imperative that in the learning stages of this work that one learns not to pretend to feel sensations that are not there. Each moment is checked for the truth.

Do I feel it or don't I? Do I hear it or don't I? These questions and ones like them are incorporated in the initial sensorial work. If you don't feel it, then you admit that you don't and move on to the next moment. When you work this way, you develop the ability to recognize the sensorial sensations that will be useful for acting. Through trial and error, you find your sensory, reality keys, and after you have worked consistently for quite some time, the sensorial response becomes instantaneous.

The general rule of thumb for making a sense-memory choice is to choose something that has occurred at least seven years in your past. I was taught, and I have found through my own experience, that the further back you go, the more reliable the responses are for acting. If the event is from your too recent past, your sense memory is too volatile, and you cannot depend on it for a professional acting experience. Very traumatic events should be handled with extreme caution and sometimes are too crippling to use in the acting technique. You must always remember that in acting you have to be able to repeat; experiencing something fully once is only the beginning. You have to find the key to a re-creation. For my students who are twenty and under, I allow a five-year window because of the limitations their youth places on their experience.

LISTENING TO MUSIC FROM MEMORY

Here is a good exercise to begin expanding you listening skills. Most people have done a form of this exercise many times in their lives, only this time, it is done with structure and for the purpose of eventually being able to use the results for acting in front of a camera.

In the case of the scene from *Casablanca*, the actors are listening to the same song that the audience hears, and that song is important to the film. This is a literal usage of listening to music. It isn't always that way. Sometimes, an actor will use listening to a song from memory, because it isn't clear what the actual music that will be used in the final edit of the film will be. Listening to a song from memory can also be used as an effect for a certain emotional condition or state. We are all quite familiar with how music connected to memories can instantaneously evoke the feelings of the time that we connect to the music. To use this kind of emotional response for acting, it must be reliable and, therefore, more consciously construed.

The music that you choose for this exercise should be something that means something to you. You should choose a song or piece of music that you strongly identify with from at least seven years ago. If you are twenty years of age or younger, five years ago will do.

1 Lie down in a comfortable position, preferably the floor, and play the piece of music that you have chosen. Listen to it. Don't get carried away by emotion or the visual memory of what the music evokes. Instead, concentrate on observing the physical sensations of hearing and how it affects the rest of your body.

2 Play the same piece several times (if it is a very long piece, than select a short excerpt of a few minutes). Just lie still, relax, and breathe. Closing your eyes or doing this in a darkened room can help the concentration.

3 Get up and start moving around the room, checking your whole body for pockets of tension. Release the tension through movement or sound while the music is playing. This is not necessarily dancing to the music, but it may start out that way. Pay particular attention to the physical effects that occur, a tightness in the pit

of your stomach for instance, and how you might release this feeling.

4 Now, turn off the music and lie back down on the floor. Go back to the relaxation and breath. Try to hear the music playing in your ears. Don't sing or hum it; hear it. Hear it playing from memory in your head. Concentrate on the ears and the inner canal of the ear.

5 Don't worry if you're not able to do this as easily as you might have thought. Unless you are a trained musician, it may be more difficult to achieve than you might have imagined. Just go back and listen more carefully. Feel the sensations inside of the ear as the music plays. Concentrate on the part of the ear that catches the sound, and feel the sound as it moves into the ear. A piece of advice: Don't play the music too loud. It's best to play it softly; it forces you to listen more closely. Loud music overwhelms the ears, and you won't be able to feel the subtle sensations that different types of sounds cause. It is these subtle vibrations that will recall the music to your memory later. Keep the face, head, and upper body as relaxed as possible. As always, keep breathing.

6 Once you have obtained even a fraction of the music in your memory and you are able to hear it without singing or humming it, you can start moving around again. You needn't hear large segments of the music, just a snippet will suffice. Changing position and moving the body should be done carefully once you have this small segment, because a sense memory is very delicate at first, and every change affects its power. Sometimes, movement enhances its strength; sometimes, it will completely diminish it, so always check to see if you can re-create the sounds you are trying to hear in your memory as you move. It's like putting on suntan lotion; you have to keep applying it as you increase activity or go swimming.

7 When the music seems reliably in your memory, move around the room and start playing with the volume of the music and direction that it's coming from. This is a tricky concept initially. Intellectually, we know that the sound is in your memory and, therefore, will always be inside of your head, but sense memory is only effective if it can be projected and expressed to communicate either your surroundings or your inner state to other people.

For some people, doing this is a natural extension of the exercise; for others, it creates confusion. Whatever it does, always express the moment truthfully and continue the exercise. There is never only one way of doing sense memory; each person's experience and expression of it is unique. That's the whole point.

8 Make the music play softly, as if it were coming from another room. Listen carefully, and allow the checking process to create the reality that you are trying to hear something of which you are not certain. Ask yourself:

- Do I hear it or don't I?

- Where is it coming from?

- Is it really coming from the room outside this one or not?

- Wonder about who is playing it and why.

It is in this checking process that the acting of a given circumstance with a sense memory begins to take place. The same checking process that you use to check the reality of a given sensorial response extends to creating a larger environment outside of yourself. If you work this way, your work becomes believable to an audience. You may have overly demonstrative reactions to the checking process at first, but as time goes by you will gain more control, and the reactions will become smaller, but more powerful and clear.

9 As you move within your space, see if you can play with the volume by using "if." If the music were coming from the other room, how loud would it be? Allow your sense of hearing to answer for you. If I move closer to the direction that the music is coming from, how much louder does it get? Allow your ears to tell you. Pose the question, and wait for the answer.

I think it is useful to watch animals, like dogs or cats, and observe how they use their listening skill. Their sense of hearing is more finely tuned than ours, and their ears can do things that ours can't, like adjust their direction to better pick up the sound vibrations, but we can easily observe how sound affects their entire bodies and well-being. I love to watch a dog eagerly waiting by the door, whimpering and trembling because the master is coming home. The dog is reacting to its sense of hearing, and what that transmits to the dog creates pure and unimpaired physical response. The dog's response to its sensorial input is always very clear to observe. There is a lot that we can learn from watching animals, particularly in the immediacy of their moment-to-moment reality.

LISTENING TO MUSIC FOR CHARACTER STUDY

Listening to music for character study can be a lot of fun, as well as being very useful for creating character response and atmosphere. As I have repeatedly stated, the film medium requires subtle gesture, and the gesture created by simply listening to music from memory is just about the right size for the close frames used in film. Whether or not this exercise will work for you in a professional situation depends on your talent and personal preferences, but it is a good exercise to do to develop listening skills while doing other tasks.

If you have recently chosen a character to work on in the exercises, then the music you chose for the listening exercise is probably already related to that character. The subconscious usually works that way; it makes connections and choices that are best for what we are trying to do at the moment. If you don't feel that the music you chose has anything to do with your character, check again, and try to put the two together. Often, there are pathways that you wouldn't have chosen consciously; your conscious choice would have been too literal and probably less powerful and interesting. The music you have chosen may make you feel things that could be an underlying key to the character's motivation. Sense-memory choices often construct a logic of their own, and even though everything is of our creation, we have to study it carefully to see how it all comes together.

For instance, if your character is a very confident and strong person, who never shows any fear or indecision, and the music you have worked on makes you feel small and insecure, you may find a way to put these two opposing elements together to create a much more complex character. If we see a person struggling to overcome her insecurities by sallying forth in a display of strength, it becomes more interesting to us. We must see the conflict in the subtle, small gesture of the face and thought patterns. It may not be in the text or action of the script. If we go back to *Casablanca* and Bogie's great scene of listening to "As Time Goes By," we see his conflict and anguish. This film allows us to hear the song as well, but what if it were a different movie, with the actor alone in his room, or a close-up of him in a crowd, and he was supposed to show the same sort of conflicting, wounded reaction, only in this film there is no central song to cue us in? The audience hears the moving sounds of the sound track that is laid down on the film long after the actor has finished his job. The actor shooting the scene is alone with the quiet sounds of a set while the camera is rolling. It is a sound of almost complete silence. There are many things that actors can use to create these kinds of private windows that they are often called upon to perform in film. Listening to music as a sense memory is one of them.

LISTENING TO THE OTHER ACTOR

In life, some of us are good listeners and some of us aren't. Sometimes, the circumstances cause us to listen up, and sometimes, we just turn off. In life, we hear what people are saying to us selectively, depending on our interest, but as an actor, and particularly as a screen actor, you must always listen with every fiber of your body. Even if you don't appear to be listening, you must be, not only to hear your cues for your next line or action, but also to give the response that is needed for the next moment. Actors can decide to some degree beforehand what their responses will be to any given cue, but the response must come directly out of the previous moment in order to create a cohesive performance. In order to do that, they must be listening to the other actors and listening to themselves, to their own inner thoughts.

Film scenes are shot in multiple takes, starting from the widest angle, the establishment shot, to the tightest angle, the close-up and extreme close-up. Most scenes are broken down into many fragments, and the actors keep repeating the same lines and moves, both physical and emotional, with the camera demanding more and more intimate exposure as it comes in closer and closer. Often, when an actor is seen in close-up, her partner in the scene may not even be on the set. The actor being filmed is looking at a red dot that is placed on the camera as her sight line, and a production assistant is blankly reading her cue lines. This creates the difficulty of acting by yourself, while appearing to be in the middle of a scene. It is perhaps the most difficult thing to do in film acting, and those that accomplish it to great effect are usually the ones we remember in a movie. It takes amazing self-knowledge to do this effectively. It also takes the courage to have an extended confrontation with yourself. In order to do that, you must be able to listen to your own inner thoughts and impulses.

Considering that a scene that lasts five minutes on the screen may take all day to shoot, how do actors prepare for this heightened form of listening? There are always many paths to the same results, but the following exercise may help you in creating and then exploring the muscles that enable you to withstand long periods of time where you are listening to someone speak and listening to your own thoughts.

JOURNAL WRITINGS AS INNER MONOLOGUE

You can do the following exercise alone, but it is most effective when done in a group. Even if you don't have an acting class or program available to you, there usually are people that you know who would be willing participants. Actors and people who want to act tend to seek out one another and form groups. I've seen it happen everywhere. People who love acting always find one another.

If you must do this exercise alone, then it should be done as though there were people there watching you. I will get into the specific techniques of doing this in chapter 6.

WORKING IN FRONT OF A GROUP

Everyone in the group is always working, whether you are the actor in front, in what I call the Hot Seat, or are a member of the group observing. The group serves as *participating observers*, and not as an audience that can sit back and think, "Okay, show me what you can do." The members of the group have a responsibility to observe and be there for the actor working in front of them. If you are in the Hot Seat, you shouldn't feel as though you are up against judges. If you do feel that way, it should be because of your own psyche, not because the group is sitting back in judgment. The circle of concentration encompasses the entire group, as if everyone were in the scene. This doesn't mean that as a member of the group, you give up your own individuality. On the contrary, you work on your own relaxation, breathing, and listening to your own inner thoughts, just as diligently as the actor working in front of you.

1 Sit alone in the Hot Seat, in front of the group, holding your Journal. The group watches and makes eye contact with you.

2 Choose a section from your Journal that is private. It could be what you have written during the Observation exercise, a diary entry (once actors have a Journal, they tend to write in them often), or it could be

your self-assessment that you've written after an exercise. What it is doesn't really matter, as long as it's private and difficult to reveal.

3 Start to read aloud from the section that you have chosen, and maintain eye contact with the other actors observing you. Stop reading aloud when you feel you are coming to the part that you don't want to reveal.

4 Read this segment to yourself, and then look up, make eye contact, and think about what you have just read and why you don't want to reveal it. Allow yourself to think as you breathe and look at someone. Try to connect.

5 Don't be afraid to use some of the relaxation and breathing techniques to relax and concentrate in front of the group. Use sighing and making the AHHH sounds to release tension.

6 Have an extended confrontation with yourself internally while you are in front of the group. Connect with what you feel.

7 The idea is to work through your Journal writings as you did with the text of the character from the previous chapter. The Inner Monologue is now spoken only to yourself. You are thinking your thoughts while you are looking at the group. Keep checking your relaxation and breathing. Try to be honest.

8 After about ten minutes, the members of the group ask you, the actor in the Hot Seat, questions. If there is a leader or teacher, he or she should moderate this section. The questions should be of a supportive nature, like, "How do you feel sitting up there?" or of a very simple nature, like, " What did you have for breakfast this morning?" You should answer while still being connected to your own inner monologue. Avoid extended answers or complicated questions. Keep it simple. The idea now is to stay connected to your inner state while saying simple words.

9 Each member of the group takes a turn in the Hot Seat. Enough time should be allotted for everyone to take a turn in one session.

In some ways, acting in front of a camera exposes who we are and breaks it down to smaller, slower parts. The personality gets deconstructed, fragmented, with the actor exposing, in a way, who she is and how she thinks. The above exercise is a good way to become more comfortable with this task and develop strong "muscles" for it.

CASABLANCA

If we go back to the movie *Casablanca* and watch the scenes where the patrons of Rick's start singing the "Marseille" to drown out the German's song, you will see more wonderful examples of listening. Here, the music, once again, takes on an important role in the film's story, but beyond that, we see each person hearing the music, then listening to his own thoughts and making a clear decision how to respond. This film sequence is rich with examples of both literal and metaphoric listening.

The last scenes of *Casablanca* that take place at the airport are wonderful examples of the classic breakdown of a scene in traditional filmmaking. For the purposes of observing listening, one should take note of whom the camera is concentrating on. We are not always watching the one who is speaking. More often than not, we are watching the one who is being spoken to; we are watching the one who is listening. In Ingrid Bergman's close-ups, as she listens to Rick explain why he's not leaving with her, she is listening to so much more that just what he is saying. We see her taking in what is being said and going through her own conflict and decision-making process. How she as an actress accomplishes this is unknown to us, but it is clear that she is having an extended confrontation with herself as she listens.

APOCALYPSE NOW

Another of my favorites films for watching actors' performances is Francis Ford Coppola's *Apocalypse Now* (both the original and the redux versions). The opening sequence of this film has Martin Sheen alone in a room in a Saigon hotel. We hear "The End," by The Doors, playing on the sound track and Captain Willard's voice-over keying us in on the story and his inner monologue. Here, we see Martin Sheen listening on many, many levels. He is listening to the sounds that he imagines he hears, and he reacts to them. He is listening to the sounds that are really in the room and reacts to them. He is clearly listening to the thoughts in his head and reacts and responds to them as well. There is no question that this actor executes an amazing feat of an extended confrontation with himself and expresses his responses to the fullest extent. In order to turn in a performance of this caliber, the actor must have incredible commitment, self-knowledge, and above all, courage. In this particular film, the actor took it to such an extent that he suffered a heart attack shortly thereafter.

Hearts of Darkness, shot by Eleanor Coppola, the director's wife, is an excellent documentary on the making of *Apocalypse Now*. I would highly recommend watching this film to anyone who wants to act in movies.

Although it is certainly an extreme case of the moviemaking scenario, it is not far from the truth of any moviemaking experience to lesser and greater degrees. In this documentary, the first scene, the genesis and process of the film, is discussed in detail. You are also able to see the outtakes (film not used in the movie) and how they developed these images into the finished product. I would suggest you watch one of the two versions of *Apocalypse Now*, think about it for at least a few days, then watch *Hearts of Darkness*. The relevance of watching these two films will speak for itself.

In this last chapter, I have tried to lay down the structure you set up for choosing, working on, and using sense memory for screen acting and the importance of the skill of listening. When we listen, we encourage a response. This process of listening and responding is greatly magnified by the fact that it is photographed in the larger-than-life formats of filmmaking.

All sensory work uses the same structure and process; you just focus the concentration on different elements. In the next chapter, we'll expand the sensory work to the realm of the skin and begin to explore the myriad possibilities of the "overall."

THE SKIN AND THE OVERALL

So, here's the movie scene: An actress walks down a cobblestone alley at night, the bare white skin of her back and arms glistening in the street lamp's glow as she slithers down the street in her little black dress and high-heeled shoes. She sees the man she loves, and the camera lingers on her face. We see that she is torn between running to him and running away from him. He sees her, and they approach one another. They argue about something that has happened earlier that evening. They look like they might start hitting one another. It's very emotional, and instead of hitting one another, they start kissing passionately. They decide to go home together, and they walk arm in arm in the moonlight. It is all beautifully shot and very romantic. As we watch them from the comfort of our chair, we engage in the fantasy of the beautiful lovers on the screen. We take part in their passion and longing, but we do not take part in their reality as screen actors.

The scene probably took twelve to fourteen hours to shoot. It is an exterior shot (filmed outside) and was originally scheduled to be shot in late August. Due to various conflicts of time and money, it is now being shot in early November. The movie takes place in the summer, so the wardrobe and atmosphere reflect the appropriate weather conditions. On the night of the actual shoot, it is forty degrees and very damp. The actors are freezing, especially the actress, stunning in her fashionable, short, backless cocktail dress and high heels. After about an hour of shooting, her feet are numb, and when the camera is not rolling, she shivers under the coat the wardrobe mistress has on hand for her, as she stands beside a portable gas heater that the production assistant has placed there. The director and the camera crew wear parkas and flannel, clothing appropriate to the weather. Sure, there is a place for her to go to, to get warm between setups, but she cannot go there between takes. She must stay close to the set, ready to step in front of the camera, into the world of the warm summer's night filled with passion, conflict, and delight.

If for no other reason than to use on a night of filming like the one described, you should learn the sense memory series of the Overall. You could use one of these sense memories to cloak yourself in the imaginary warmth of a summer's night and keep your concentration on the scene, instead of on the fact that you are freezing. If you have learned how to engage your skin in the realms of your sensorial imagination, then you will be able to create the body language appropriate to a warm summer's night, rather than that of an actor going numb with cold.

THE OVERALL

We are encased in the largest organ of our bodies, our skin. The skin has two layers, the outer layer, called the epidermis, which has no feelings, and the inner layer, sometimes called the true skin, which is highly vascular and sensitive. We will be dealing with this highly sensitive and vascular part of the skin's qualities in this chapter and how it can be used in the sense memory series of the Overall.

An Overall is a condition that can be experienced *over all* of the surface of the skin at one time. It also includes the sympathetic reactions that these conditions cause in the rest of the body. The best example of an Overall is nakedness. Nakedness is the ultimate Overall, because it is a condition that is clearly experienced over the entire surface of the skin and certainly creates sympathetic reactions in the rest of the body. Many things that we do naked are also a part of this sense memory series like shower, bath, sauna, and steam room. Weather conditions are also Overalls, conditions like rain, sunshine, wind, or extreme cold. All of these conditions are external conditions that are experienced over the surface of the skin through the sensation of touch. When used literally, the creation of these external conditions through sense memory can be very useful for an atmosphere that may be necessary in a film scene, as in the example I mentioned above. Metaphorically, they can be used to create a character or a reaction needed for a specific shot. It is the metaphoric aspect of these sense memories that makes them of special interest.

I will give you several different examples of an Overall and explain how to create a sense memory on the skin. Once you have done one or two Overalls, it is easy to take on others, as the system of creating each one is similar.

NAKEDNESS

As I said before, nakedness is the ultimate Overall and, therefore, a good place to start. If you have never done this type of exercise before, you should be aware that almost anything can happen. It is also possible that nothing happens or that your reactions are minimal. Each person has strengths and weaknesses when it comes to sense memory, which means that there are people for whom certain exercises do almost nothing. If you find that to be the case with one Overall, try another. If none of them work for you, go on to something else. Always give yourself at least two two-hour sessions of working on an exercise before you decide that it's not working for you.

To begin working on Nakedness, you must of course start, as always, with the Relaxation.

1 Do the Mental Relaxation exercises for about twenty minutes.

2 When you are ready to start to focus your concentration, stand up and turn your focus to the parts of your body that tend to be naked all the time. That would generally be your face, your hands, your neck, possibly your arms, and very often your feet and parts of your legs.

3 Pick one part of the body, like a naked arm for instance, and concentrate on the skin and how it feels being exposed to the air. Move the arm in space slowly, while keeping the breath high in the chest.

4 Once you have a sense of your skin being naked on that arm, move to the other parts of your body that are also naked, like your cheeks and forehead, and try to discern the same feeling of nakedness that you felt on your arm.

5 Take the sensation that you can identify on your naked skin, and start to move your concentration to the skin surfaces that are beneath your clothes. If you start with the portion of your arm that is naked, then move slowly up the arm to the shoulder that is covered by the cloth of your shirt. First, you feel the skin and the cloth touching it—the actual reality must be accepted first—then move the sensation of nakedness that you pinpointed on the actual naked skin to the area of skin in the shoulder area which is covered by clothing.

6 Move very slowly in this process, starting with a shoulder and moving slowly down the back. The checking process is incorporated into this exercise by the comparison of sensations on the truly naked skin to the area of skin that you are focusing on. The

question that is posed is: If this is how the skin on my naked hand feels in reality, how would that sensation feel if it was the skin on my lower back? If this is how the skin on my cheek feels, then how would it feel if it was the skin on my inner thigh? And so on.

7 The object is a "connect the dots" game. The parts of the body that are naked all the time in public are taken for granted in the western world; we don't even think of these parts as being naked, but they are. If we can connect this feeling of nakedness over the entire body, we have the beginnings of this exercise.

8 The more private the part of the body, the harder it is to achieve the sensation of nakedness. Remember, though, that the state of nakedness is self-explanatory: no clothing at all. In order to achieve this state, we must concentrate on the skin over every part of our bodies, including the genitalia. It should not be an easy process, but rather one laden with all kinds of surprises.

9 The body must be in constant motion while working on Nakedness, especially the part of the body on which your attention is focused. The movement is not large, but it is movement all the same. You should avoid becoming stiff or overwhelmed by the sensation. When my students start to connect to a sensation and begin allowing that sensation to travel to different parts of their bodies, they tend to become afraid of moving their bodies. They are under the impression that movement will dissipate the sensation. They have to learn how to deepen the concentration, so that movement deepens the sensation and makes it more reliable. I always tell them they look like the extras in *Night of the Living Dead*. Sensory work should be fluid and alive, not stiff and zombie-like. Only if it is fluid can it be used for acting purposes.

You may ask yourself, why work on something like Nakedness in the first place? At first, you work on an exercise like this to develop your sensory instrument, so that it will respond to your imagination more fully when it is given a command. An exercise like Nakedness incorporates the whole of the body; no area can be left out. As an actor, you are able to literally explore every inch of your external self and discover what kinds of responses are there for you to use for future reference.

An exercise like Nakedness could make you feel very confident and sexual. It could take away your inhibitions and make you move in a way that would normally elude you. This way of movement could be used to create the basic movement of a character. On the other hand, Nakedness could make you feel shy and intimidated, which could also be used for the basic movement for a character. It doesn't matter what the reactions are, what is important is that they be truthful, consistent, and reliable. In order to get a response that is reliable, you have to work on the exercise for at least two weeks.

The basic movement of the character is an inner rhythm that is always present. This basic movement is not necessarily the character's walk or grimace or a gesture that one associates with a theatrical performance. It is a much more subtle movement, an internal rhythm or "music" to which the character always moves. An Overall is an excellent way to begin to create this basic movement of a character.

SUNSHINE

Sunshine is one of the most popular sense memories, and one that everyone seems to be able to do very easily. Most of us associate the sun with good times, and we go into the exercise with expectations of pleasure, but Sunshine can be many things.

1 First, decide from which direction the sun is coming. Is it directly above you or on an angle in front of you? Place the sun in a realistic relationship to yourself.

2 Decide with which part of your body you are going to start, and place that part in direct line with your imaginary sun source. I would suggest the hands or the face, preferably a cheek, which is the example that I will use. First, you must feel the sensations of the skin as it exists in the moment. To help you to do this, you centralize the area that you are working on. For instance, to centralize your concentration on your left cheek, begin by concentrating on your eyeballs and moving them around in their sockets. Now, concentrate only on the left eye. You know that your left cheek is just below your left eye, so move the concentration down from the eye to the cheek. Wriggle you nose, and feel its bone structure with your concentration (it's best not to touch yourself with your hands, but rather to direct the concentration mentally). You know that your left cheek is to the left of your nose, so again, move the concentration to the left cheek. Be very specific when you centralize an area to begin working on it: below the left eye, left of the nose, etc. Don't assume you know

where something is—direct the concentration there without touching or looking at it.

3 Now, add the memory of sunshine to the area that you have specified and centralized. It should be very hot sunshine. Move the area around in the rays of your imaginary sun. Breathe into the sensations and impulses that occur as a result of this attempt.

4 Avoid sun-like behavior. In other words, do not take on the body language of someone who is sitting in the sun, e.g., lounging, relaxed on the beach, sunbathing while on vacation, etc. None of that has anything to do with the Sunshine exercise. An Overall is a sensation on the skin, not a place. For some people, it takes a lot of concentration to separate the sensations of sun on the skin from the places with which they associate this activity in their minds. It's important to separate the two experiences.

5 If you can feel the sun on your cheek, move the sensation to another area of the body, and see what happens. Keep moving the sensation of sun on the skin, until you find the area that has the greatest response. It could be anywhere on your body. For some people, the sun can be felt most intensely on their backs; for others, it may be their toes. It doesn't matter where it is. What matters is that you feel the response and it is truthful. Once a response is truthful, you can usually depend on recreating it again and again.

The sensation of sunshine is thought of by most people to be used as a weather condition for acting. If it is supposed to be a sunny environment, the actor acts like they are in the sun. They squint their eyes, lick their lips from thirst, and wipe away the sweat from their brow. All of these things would be called indicating. You use a gesture to indicate what is going on in the environment. These gestures are generally too stagey for the camera. Unless you are performing in high comedy, such indication of reality should be avoided by the screen actor. Although Sunshine could be used for the literal purpose of being in the sun, it is not the ultimate sense memory purpose of Sunshine.

Sunshine, like Nakedness, can have a myriad of affects on one who uses it as part of a character development. The response is so individual and the usage so broad that I could not describe it all here, except to say that each person creates the work anew and takes it further into the realm of unique creativity. Sense memory is a little like learning a new language; it is accumulative knowledge. Many things that make no sense whatsoever today will become perfectly clear and understandable tomorrow.

OTHER OVERALL EXAMPLES

BATH

Bath is a great overall to do if you are experiencing a great deal of tension and pressure. You can do Bath either in a chair or by lounging on the floor with your back against the wall. Bath can be used for many states of mind that an actor may not be personally familiar with, like being very stoned or drunk. The Overall sense memory of Very Hot Bath could produce a drugged state.

Seat yourself in a chair and lean back. Imagine that you are immersed in hot water up to your neck, your head leaning comfortably on the side of the tub. Start from the top of your neck, and work your way down your body. Try and feel the water all over your skin, as well as the smooth tub on your back and legs. Take your hand, and hold it in front of you. See if you can feel the weight of the water and the buoyancy your hand would have if it were in the bath. Avoid creating the bathroom and moving into place. Try to stay within the realm of the sense of touch. You might try bringing in the sense of hearing and listen to the sound of the water as you move within the bath. Bringing in this sound often helps to create the whole bath experience.

SAUNA/STEAM ROOM

If you are not in the habit of going to the sauna or steam room regularly, then this is not a good exercise for you. The general rule is, only work with what you know. However, if you are a fan of either the sauna or steam room, this can be an excellent Overall.

First, choose which of the two you are going to work on. Once you have chosen, start by feeling the heat and how it affects your breathing, the hot air coming into your lungs and the quality of that air. It is moist if it's the steam room and dry if it's the sauna. The heat of these places causes the body to be under a certain type of pressure, which makes it difficult to move and speak. Try to recreate the feeling of the sweat beading on your skin or rolling down the small of your back.

You can bring the sense of smell into this exercise. Most saunas or steam rooms have a very specific odor, which you should try to isolate as you breathe in the hot air. The sound of the hissing steam or the coals coming on can also help to create the sensation on the skin. Avoid creating the place, and stay with the sensations on the skin, aided by the sense of hearing and smell.

The Skin and the Overall

Don't forget to create the feeling of the benches or tiles of the sauna/steam room on your skin if you need to incorporate that to get the feeling of the heat. If you can accomplish the sensations of any condition for an Overall on your skin without moving into the other senses, then you should just stay with the sensations of touch. Never complicate matters more than necessary. If your instrument responds fully with very little stimulus, consider yourself lucky, and move forward with a character or text.

Sauna/Steam Room can be a very interesting choice if you must tell someone something that is very difficult for you to tell them. It can also be used if you have a secret that is difficult for you to reveal or if you must admit to something you are ashamed of. These sense memories are meant to be a jump-start in the acting technique to help you be connected to truthful behavior. It doesn't matter what the element of truth is—the camera is not a judge—but the truth must be there in some form, otherwise the camera, in its objectivity, sees the lie.

RAIN AND WIND

The use of these two elements, either separately or together, produces very powerful results in some people. There are many combinations that can be used. Whatever you choose to do, be clear about your choice. For instance, you can use warm rain and soft wind, or strong cold wind alone, or cold rain with strong wind, etc.—you get the picture. You can also work on one separately. You work on Rain and Wind the same way that you work on Nakedness or Sunshine. You centralize an area of skin, and then work on releasing the sensorial memory of the condition that you have chosen. You work slowly and systematically to "connect the dots" of the sensation on the areas of skin that respond to the sense memory.

When working on these Overalls, avoid moving the exercise into a place. As with Sunshine, the exercise should stay within the realm of your skin and not move into scenarios of places and events. In the initial stages of this work, you have to be certain to contain the exercise in order to discipline the concentration. Later, as you progress in this work, you can start combining sense memories and creating spaces.

SCENARIOS THAT INVADE YOUR CONCENTRATION

When a place or scenario (a memory of a particular event) comes up during the Overall exercise, you should acknowledge that it is occurring, but not get involved in pursuing the imagination further into the story. Keep going back to the sensations of the skin and the proliferation of the Overall on the skin. The Inner Monologue is an excellent way of acknowledging an invading place or scenario. Use the Inner Monologue to express the frustration and difficulty that you have concentrating on your objective—feeling the sun on your skin. Physical movement such as "shaking it out" or jumping up and down can also help an errant concentration get back on track. If you drop your Overall, shake it out, then begin again. You would go back to the last thing that you were connected to, the last thing that worked before you got distracted by a story or place.

It is imperative to train the concentration to stay with that which you have directed it to do and not allow it to wander through the whole of your subconscious at will. There's nothing wrong with letting the concentration wander around like that if you are just sitting somewhere and musing at the sky, but it is generally a waste of time for an actor, because it is too intro-spective and self-absorbed. It's not a productive sense memory that one can draw from and use for a character in a professional acting environment. It's just self-indulgent mind play, which has to be done on your free time, not when you are working.

If you find yourself wandering too much during an exercise and cannot keep your concentration focused even though you try, there may be some things that you need to fix. One is, the sense memory choice may be connected to something that is too traumatic for your emotional state and, therefore, useless to you as an actor. You may need to make a differ-ent choice or move to a different type of exercise altogether. We must listen to ourselves, and when the system comes under stress, it usually notifies us by taking us far away from the dangerous area, or it keeps bringing us back to the same place over and over again. If the latter occurs, it is because there is something that needs to be discovered in that place and is useful. Often, we will have to compartmentalize such a space and make a note that this place will have to be fully investigated in the future. Set time aside to do this work, but don't allow it to invade an exercise to which you have already directed your concentration. If you allow yourself to wander like that, you will never develop the discipline needed to use sense memory as an actor.

Another thing to consider if you find yourself wandering into foreign terrain when doing an exercise is that you may need more time to just daydream, or you may simply need more sleep. When I first started doing sense memory, I found myself falling asleep over and over again. I would start an exercise, get going, be really relaxed, and the next thing I knew, I'd be waking up from a deep, deep sleep two hours later, and half of my body was numb from the strange position that I was curled up in. When I told my teacher, Walter Lott, that this was happening, he would say, "Well,

Catherine, I guess that's just what you need to do right now before you can get to the next step." Great, I thought, what the hell is that supposed to mean? I didn't realize at the time that I was completely exhausted, and given the opportunity to relax and clear my mind, my organism stole those hours to put me to sleep. If you are not rested, you will not be able to work efficiently. Acting requires enormous strength.

DOES IT REALLY WORK?

The Overalls, and all sense memories, should be worked on extensively. Each time you work on an Overall, you investigate deeper and deeper into your own acting instrument. Somewhere deep within, there are keys or triggers that bring back the whole experience and make it easier to be connected to the basic rhythm of your character. After you have, say, sunshine on the whole of your body, you might need only to recall in truth a tiny piece of sunny warmth on your palm in order to bring back a whole experience and, thereby, an essential underlying element of a character. The easy access of the Overall makes it very popular with screen actors.

You will find that many actors will deny using such methods in their work. They will say things like, I used to do all that sense memory stuff, but I don't anymore, because it slows me down. In fact, many of these actors studied sense memory for many years and learned all of the exercises and how to use them in character development. Now, as working, professional actors, their responses are instantaneous, and they no longer must invest the time for sense memory exercises. Their instrument is already attuned to being alive with sensorial input, and they act with the full faculty of their five senses, their entire bodies, and their imagination.

The truth is that if they hadn't done all the years of work that they now claim to have discarded, they would not have the richness of response that they have at their fingertips today. Many movie stars who claim to have no acting technique hire private coaches who put them through their paces and help them to develop the characters with the sensorial and emotional work that they will need to film the part. These coaches are rarely given credit and almost never spoken of, but they exist, and most of them come from this very rich line of training in sensory work and emotional memory.

I cannot stress enough how individual this work is and that no stock response is expected for any exercise. You just have to be connected to your own concentration and imagination to see where it leads you. An Overall can be so powerful that it can ground a character in a way that is really indescribable. Comprehensive work on an Overall can create the same essence of a character over and over again and, most importantly, over the passage of time. Films, no matter what their budgets, often get shot inconsistently and over long periods of time. It's possible that after a film has been completed, the director or producer decides to change whole sections. These sections will have to be reshot. It could be a year or more since the film was wrapped, so you should have some mechanism for making sure the character will be cohesive. A small section of an Overall can work miracles in this situation, providing, of course, that it was integrated into the original shoot to begin with.

The next chapter will begin to deal with the space outside of yourself, as we begin to explore whom we are speaking to when we speak to the camera and how to create an imaginary partner through Substitution.

SUBSTITUTION: THE CAMERA AS PARTNER

Substitution, by definition, is putting a person or thing in the place of another to perform the same duties, as in a substitute teacher. It implies that the one that was there before is no longer present and needed to be replaced. In acting, we are constantly substituting our own life and experiences for the given circumstances of the script in order to increase our understanding and gain the sense of reality that we need to act our parts. However, in acting, the given circumstances and characters of the script are still present; we are substituting our own circumstances only temporarily. We do this to gain insight into the behavior and reactions of the character by recalling our own parallel experiences. Once we have this insight we must blend it with the action of the script. All actors do this, either consciously or unconsciously. We do this to build our confidence and give us the feeling that we are navigating through familiar territory. Actors need confidence in order to take the risk to discover new things about their parts. Having a basis in their own reality helps them attain this confidence.

SUBSTITUTION FOR A PERSON
In this chapter, I will refer to substitution only in relation to people. The technique, which I will call Substitution, is interfacing the other characters in the script with people that you know from your own life. This technique is used in all kinds of acting, but is essential in film acting, where so much of the time, the actor stands alone before the camera, lights blocking out any view but the blackness of the lens, and acts. The actor is essentially acting with the camera as his or her partner. This relationship must be a love affair.

The camera is, after all, just a machine—it is cold and objective, it has no feelings, no opinions, nor points of view. How, then, do you create the necessary world to which you are reacting in order to act with the camera? Sure, you have the work that you have done with your partners from the scene, you have what the director has told you, and you have what you have told yourself—all these things will give you a certain amount of fuel for acting with the camera. In order to keep the process of moment-to-moment reality alive, you need to have created an alive presence with which to interact, a presence that will be feeding you impulses and inspiring your imagination. This presence is your Substitution.

SUBSTITUTION AND FILMMAKING

Substitution can and should be used at all phases of your work on a character. It should be called upon as needed when you don't understand what you are doing or cannot find the *spark* that you need to ignite a difficult scene. In film acting, where the scene will be deconstructed into many different angels and camera takes, the fuel you need for doing one shot, where you are acting with other actors in the scene, is very different from the fuel you need to do a close-up reaction shot or monologue, as you stand alone talking only to the camera. Actors are never told beforehand what the coverage is going to be on a scene. (Coverage is the term used for how a scene will be photographed, i.e., how many shots, from what angles, and of whom.) I am not sure why this is. I suppose it's because many times, the director doesn't know how he is going to shoot it himself until shortly before he does it. Even though the shots may have been planned, the nature of good filmmaking is allowing the creation of a collaborative work to flourish on the set with the actors. It is a continuation of the moment-to-moment reality that extends to the director and crew. Directors who are able to be prepared, command a crew, and still leave space for spontaneity and creativity when the actors walk on a set are usually considered great, because it is a very difficult thing to do.

So what happens when the actor is lucky enough to work with a great director and is now called upon spontaneously to act out many subtle and fragmented aspects of the scene? An experienced film actor has a whole bag of Substitutions that she can pull up at any time when needed. You never know what will arise during a scene and what kind of coverage the director may choose to have for it. If what you are doing in the scene is interesting, then the director may spontaneously choose to cover you more than previously planned. You have to be ready for your close-up; you have to have Substitutions waiting in the wings.

Substitution is very tricky business. It is very often misunderstood, and when such a technique is misunderstood, it can really sow the seeds of bad acting or, in the very least, acting that is removed and self-indulgent. The whole purpose of Substitution is to make you more connected to what and to whom you are talking. That being said, this is a technique with which one must become familiar before using it on a film set. Once you have built strength and your own style of incorporating this technique into the fabric of your acting skills, it becomes a gem to use and behold.

THE FIRST STEPS TO THE SUBSTITUTION TECHNIQUE: CHOOSING THE RIGHT SUBSTITUTE

The first step to mastering the Substitution technique is creating an imaginary person through the use of your five senses. When I say imaginary, I don't mean someone who doesn't exist, like a child that has an imaginary friend, someone that they have made up completely and who doesn't exist in reality. I mean a person who you know well and who you create in front of you with the use of your imagination and your senses.

As with any sense memory, the choice of what, or in this case whom, to work on is essential. The person that you choose to create should be someone with whom you have a relationship of substance. The best people are the ones from your primal relationships, primal meaning the first people with whom you come in contact in your life, that is, people from your family structure—father, mother, sister, brother, etc.—the people who make up your household. These relationships are loaded emotionally and filled with needs and desires that were left unmet. This can make for good acting material, because you have needs that need to be fulfilled.

Sometimes, the relationships may be so loaded that to try and create these people through sense memory would only serve to infantilize you. If the relationship is too emotionally charged, it can render you powerless and unable to act. Therefore, the choice of that person should be avoided at this time.

If you allow your subconscious to make the choice for you, it will usually choose the right person for whatever you are working on at the moment. If you aren't working on anything specific, then use the character and the monologue you used in chapter 3 as a starting point. Here are some guidelines for choosing the right person to work on for a Substitute:

- Make the choice after doing the Mental Relaxation exercises for at least twenty minutes.

- Let your memory wander through your past, and focus on the people who have been part of your family and friends.

- Think of the people you have cared about, those who have made a big impression on you (positive or negative) and those you have loved.

- The relationship should be from at least seven years ago (the general sense memory rule), although you may still know the person now. They could be deceased, although be advised that you create a potentially extremely charged situation when you do this.

- The right person to choose is the first person to figure prominently in your mind.

Sense memory choices should not be belabored. You shouldn't sit around and decide on a substitution choice the way you might decide what you are going to wear to a party. The choice should be clear to you, because it is usually the first person you think of. This is always the choice that will take you from the present moment to where you want to go. It is called intuition, and actors can always intuit the best choice for the moment if they are relaxed and concentrated and have the courage to leave themselves alone.

CREATING AN IMAGINARY PERSON: SUBSTITUTION AS A SENSE MEMORY

Once you have chosen your substitute, you can begin working on the exercise. This exercise must be preceded by a long and thorough Mental Relaxation period if it is to be effectual. You will be creating an imaginary "object" that is another living human being with whom you have a complex relationship, so you need to be very relaxed in order to chart this very rich and volatile territory.

1 Place two chairs opposite one another, and sit in one of them. In your mind, place your substitute person in the other chair.

2 Keep the relaxation process going, making sure that you get plenty of air when you breathe. Make sounds, and use the Inner Monologue. Stay in the chair, and stay in the moment. Be very aware of rising tension and its release.

3 Begin to create the substitute by using your five senses. Start with vision—sight. Most people will immediately try to see the face of the person, but this may not be the easiest route to establishing imaginary reality. Although you might think you are most familiar with the face—certainly you recognize it among other faces when you see it—it is an extremely complicated canvas, with many minute details—details, by the way, that change with time. It is much easier to start with the general size and shape of the person and to start by posing questions. For instance, if my

substitute is 6'4" tall, then how high would his head be in relationship to mine if he were sitting in this empty chair opposite me? Pose the question, then allow your visual memory to answer. Continue with the rest of the body. Be specific. Question: If my substitute were sitting in this chair, where would his legs be? How far out would the knees come? Are the legs crossed? Where are the feet?

4   The next series of questions that should be posed deal with what the person is wearing. If we give our subconscious free reign, it will drop this person into our imaginary reality from a specific point in time. He will be wearing something from that time. It may be something that we recognize immediately, or we may not recognize it at all. The thing *not* to do is to say to yourself, "Oh, Sammy always wore those blue jeans and that old red plaid shirt," and then try to make yourself see him wearing that outfit. This approach will not work as an effective acting tool.

The outfit emerges slowly, piece by piece. You may only be able to realize a cuff of a shirt or a necklace that lies on the breastbone, but this may be more than enough to bring the image of the whole person clearly to your imagination in front of you.

5   Once you have a visual piece of your substitute, and indeed it need only be a piece, you can start to move to the next sense—smell. Everyone has a scent of his own. With some people, you are readily aware of their scent, a perfume or cologne that they always wore or the smell of a painter's oils. Work on your relaxation, and take in a large amount of air, as if you were smelling the ocean. As you take in the air, concentrate on your nose and the inside of your nostrils. Feel the air going in, and ask the questions: What do I smell? Is there a smell associated with this person? Do I smell it now? What do I smell? It is possible that you smell something that is related to the person, like a food that she would cook on her stove or a place that she used to take you to. You never know what your imagination will offer in response to a question. One thing that you can be sure of, though, if you ask, your imagination will give you the right answer.

6   Various aspects of the person should be clearly before you in the chair. If you have created any kind of sensory reality, you will be

very concentrated and connected to that chair where the person that your imagination has created is seated. You do not have to sit head-on to the person, nor do you have to look at her. What you do have to do is make sure that you have power over your own body. You should be able to move freely, although you remain seated. Your face remains relaxed, and you are breathing fully into each moment.

7 In the fashion of the Inner Monologue, begin to speak to your substitute. Speak in short, direct sentences or sentence fragments; do not get conversational. Don't forget that at this point, you are still doing a sense memory exercise, you are not playacting a scenario. Your body should not take on the language of, say, someone sitting in a lounge having a drink with a friend. Be very aware of small jerks or adjusted movements in the body before you speak. This indicates that you are not speaking directly from the moment in a natural and connected fashion, but that you are arranging the moment before you speak. Be very careful of the preconceived idea. We spoke about preconceived ideas in chapter 3 in relation to character. We also have preconceived ideas about ourselves and our relationships with the people in our lives. When you are working with a substitute, it is very important to allow your speech to come directly out of the moment and the inspiration that you are receiving from the imaginary object. This interaction is part of the creation process.

8 After you have spoken to your substitute for a while, it's time to work on the next sense—hearing. Go back to working on the visual and spatial imaginary reality of your substitute, and reestablish a connection through one of the other senses, either sight or smell. Do not speak during this time; be quiet and start to listen. As with any sense memory, the concentration goes to the organ that does the job, in this case, the ears. Try to connect to at least two senses at the same time. See the person, concentrate on the ears, and try to hear the voice. This is very similar to the exercise of listening to the music from memory. You direct the concentration to the ear canals and allow the sound to filter through. If you are relaxed and in the moment, you should be able to hear the voice. Keep the breath moving through the moments. It can be very emotionally intense to do this part of the exercise, and you will need your breath. Really listen to what this

person has to say to you. Listen to your own thoughts, while your body and breath react to what your substitute is saying to you.

9 Interact with your substitute without speaking, while listening and reacting to your own thoughts. This is similar to the Journal Writings as Inner Monologue Exercise of chapter 4.

MOVING THE SUBSTITUTE AROUND THE ROOM

This next exercise is a continuation of the above exercise. It can be done the first time you try the Substitution if you feel that your connection is strong enough to keep going. On the other hand, you might want to work up to it and try this exercise after you have done the previous exercise several times and you can re-create your substitute with confidence.

1 Start with twenty minutes of Mental Relaxation.

2 Place a chair opposite yours for the substitute to be in. Work on the same person as you did for the first exercise, and create her through sight, smell, and sound.

3 Once you are interacting with her, remain seated as you see her stand up and walk away from the chair that she was sitting in. Do this carefully, because it is possible that she will disappear all together. If she does disappear, go back to the last strongest sense memory you connected to the substitute, and carefully place her in the chair. Try to carefully see her getting up, carefully see her walking away.

4 Relax the space behind your eyes, as you work on seeing the substitute move. Avoid straining the eyes as a form of concentration. The greater the task for the concentration, the greater the relaxation. Seeing a person who you have created through your imagination and sensory memory walk across the room and begin to move of her own free will is a very strenuous task for the concentration. Therefore, it requires deep relaxation.

5 Place the substitute across the room somewhere. Don't speak to her, just listen to your own thoughts. You can do the Inner Monologue if you must speak.

6 Get up from your chair, and turn your back on your substitute. Feel that she is still there in the room with you by keeping one of the senses other than sight going. If your connection is very strong, you may not have to do anything to keep her presence real for you. In life, we feel the presence of those around us even when we are not directly looking at them. If we are having a conversation with someone who is in the room with us, we might be doing something other than staring directly at her. We know that she is there, even without constant eye contact. People have varying degrees of power over us, depending on their proximity. It is the same with substitutes: Once you have created them, they are there, whether you are looking at them or not.

7 Close you eyes, and reach out your hand. Have your substitute come up to you and touch your hand. Feel her hand on yours. Keep your eyes closed for now. Once you have the sensory connection of her hand on yours, slowly open your eyes and see her before you. Try to see her face. You must keep the face and eyes relaxed during this exercise. If the impulse of the sensory search is overwhelming, you can look away or walk away, but keep the connection going in a flowing and relaxed manner.

You may not want to be touched by your substitute for some reason, which is, of course, your prerogative. However, in the world of imaginary reality, this is a valid response for the sense of touch. Just as not seeing the person when your back is turned, yet still knowing that she is there, is a sensorial reality for sight, you are still interacting with your imaginary object through the use of your senses.

8 Interact with your substitute by allowing her to move at will. Do not let the touch, if you have allowed it to occur, go beyond the touching of hands. Speak to your substitute in simple, repetitive language. Ask questions. Don't dissipate your imaginary reality through conversational speech. Don't get into scenarios and places. Just stay with the sensory facts of the person and your imaginary reality with her.

9 Do your monologue to the substitute, allowing the impulses from your interaction to dictate how the monologue is said. Stay in the moment, and leave space for the discovery of something new, surprising, or unknown to take place.

LETTING GO OF THE EXERCISE

Any exercise that requires a good deal of concentration to get into should have a clear passage to get out of the depth of concentration. Particularly when you start to move into the areas of Substitution and the Room exercise of the next chapter, you must decide when you are finished with the exercise and allot time for a "cooling down" period. This is done consciously by slowly letting go of the imaginary reality piece by piece.

If you have been doing the Substitution exercise, for example, then you would let go of the person sense by sense, sight being, most likely, the last. You never create a scenario where the person exits the room and that's how your sense memory ends. In a case like that, it hasn't ended; you are still in your imaginary reality. All that you have changed is the visual presence of the Substitute. Your imagination is still connected to it.

To disengage yourself from a strong sense memory, you must replace the sense memories with sense realities. If you are working with smell, then work to smell what is truly in the room and take notice of it. Stand still, and close your eyes. Listen to the sounds in the room. Notice them. Listen to the sounds of traffic or of birds outside the room. Notice them. Feel your feet in your shoes and your shoes on the ground. Feel the clothing on your body, and touch your hands and face. Open your eyes and see the room. Look at it almost scientifically, asking questions about specific things: How high are the windows? How old is this rug? How many electrical outlets are in the room? Come back to the room you are standing in. Be aware of the sights, sounds, smells, and feelings of the present.

This is an important aspect of this work. It makes your work specific and much easier to manage and control.

FINDING THE KEY TO YOUR SUBSTITUTE

It goes without saying that you don't have time to sit and relax for twenty minutes, slowly doing the sensory steps to create your substitute, on a film set. When they call you to the set to shoot, you can't start doing your Inner Monologue, talking to the substitute that only you can see, as a way of "warming up" your imaginary reality to get you ready to act. You have to do all that work repeatedly at home on your own time. When you are on a set, you basically are expected to be prepared and to just act. What you are prepared with, what you have taken with you from your work at home, is, among other things, a set of keys that unlock the sensory experiences that are useful in a moment's notice.

The key is important to any sense memory, because it is how we apply what we have done in our own private work to our acting. The key is found while you are doing the exercise, through trial and error. While you are doing the Substitution exercise, take notice of what sensorial aspect brings the imaginary reality to an emotional connection and causes a reaction in you. This would be the starting point of the key. Sometimes, this connection may be too overpowering to act with, but you can attempt to blend this imaginary reality with your character. If it serves your acting talent and causes you to move forward, propelling you through the part, it is a good choice. If it bogs you down into a past personal experience that makes you oblivious to the actions of your part, then it needs to be either pared down (use less of the sensorial reality) or discarded for another key that serves you better.

This does not happen instantaneously. As with anything that is highly specialized and extremely subjective, it takes time to choose what aspects of your work at home should be taken to a professional environment. The short answer is, the ones that help you act your parts more easily, more fluidly, and with greater creativity. Nothing will give you an answer better than experiences that will teach you to make the right choices through trial and error.

MONOLOGUE WITH SUBSTITUTION

A good way to test choices that you have made for a Substitution is to see if you can instantaneously create your substitute with your key sense memory. Focus your concentration on the sensory key that you have chosen, and see how much of the Substitution experience it brings back. You should be emotionally connected very quickly. It isn't necessary to bring back the entire experience of the Substitution, only the portion of it that was strong for you. With time, actors learn how to gauge these things for themselves according to need.

Do a monologue as if you were speaking to your substitute. Don't worry if the given circumstances match with the person you have chosen or not; it's just an exercise. Try to connect to the words and your imaginary reality (the substitute) to create a moment-to-moment experience.

You may or may not have chosen a visual approach. In other words, it is possible to bring back the emotional and sensorial connection of your Substitution without seeing the person. Special attention, however, must be paid to the eyes in this case. The eyes need to engage, and if you are not looking at anything specific, they will wander and glaze over. This can be deadly for screen acting. Be sure that your eyes are focused on a point that could be the face of the person that you are talking to and one or several other points that your eyes can go back to. You needn't stare into the eyes of your imaginary person. You can look away, just like you do in life, but you will always have to go back to the same point of focus where the eyes would be. This must be practiced before going in front of a camera, so that it becomes an automatic technique that does not tire the eyes. Beware of blinking or fluttering the eyes. These motions are signs of tension and the lack of a direct connection to what is happening in the moment. It also looks very ugly and distracting in close-ups and must be avoided at all costs.

SPEAKING TO THE LENS

Who are we speaking to when we are speaking to the lens of a camera? There is always a logical and intellectual answer to this question—a literal answer that comes from the structure of the script. You are talking to your brother, you are talking to the troops, you are talking to your lover, you are talking directly to the audience, etc., and all these answers are easily found in the script.

What about what excites and interests you personally? What about the unique opportunity to say something directly to one person or to many people for all eternity through the camera lens? A focused, concentrated message that filters through the text of a fictional character, through the sensory process, and becomes a personal statement. In my opinion, it is one of the great pluses of filmmaking for the actor. This wonderful opportunity to express oneself directly to all can be an almost omnipotent experience, and one that shouldn't be squandered. If the audience is out there in the dark waiting to be spoken to, then we as the actors should have something to say to them. Sure the writers and directors are seemingly in control of that expression, but we are the human voices, the souls, if you would, of the message. We should use the opportunity fully, by investing ourselves fully into this endeavor with heroic glee. Movies project life on an enormous scale, and very often, the actor must be willing to address this larger-than-life scale within himself. For the camera, this cannot be done with large, sweeping gestures most of the time, but, I believe, is achieved from an almost spiritual commitment to something larger than one's self.

When given such an opportunity to speak directly to the camera, one should try and use one's highest self. I believe a level of spirituality is necessary, a belief that extends beyond one's own small scope. Through the deep connection with the self, a connection with an essence, which is a non-intellectual process, to something that cannot be expressed in words, one can come in contact with the universal. Or you could call it the spiritual.

Substituting a person you know for someone in a script is a very common practice among all actors, but learning to truly engage yourself with that person and be able to act and interact with that imaginary creation is a much more unique and difficult task. To only intellectually associate a person you know with a character in a script, who is either directly present or is only mentioned, will not give you the full benefit of the imagination and the memory. It is the physicalization of the memory through the senses that makes the Substitution particularly useful and powerful.

Creating an imaginary person also takes your imagination out of your head and into the space around you, therefore, it engages the entire body. It brings you, and the audience, into the physical world that surrounds you, the world created by the imagination. It is this imaginary world, which is made up of the remnants of one's own life, that the film actor projects into space. In the next chapter, I will go further into the concept of creating a space, as we learn to do the complex series of sense memories called Place.

CREATING THE SPACE

There is a scene in the 1994 movie, *Legends of the Fall*, that begins with Sam the Indian arguing with the Hired Hand about a broken wagon wheel. It's a slice of daily life on the ranch, mundane and familiar. Suddenly, Sam stops listening to the Hired Hand and looks out into the distance—he sees something. The Hand looks at Sam, who points into the distance. The Hand looks and sees what Sam is looking at; a man is riding towards the house. He yells out to the Colonel. The Colonel is sitting outside of the house, reading with Sam's daughter, Isabel Two. He looks into the distance, searching the horizon. Sam's wife is beating a rug. She stops and looks into the distance. The Colonel sees the man riding on a horse towards them; it is Tristan, his son, returning from the war. Susannah, the woman he left behind, is standing in the doorway, looking into the distance. Tristan is drawing nearer. The Colonel, his father, stands up and takes two steps forward. Sam walks forward, Sam's wife walks forward, and Tristan, sunlit from behind, is coming closer and closer to them.

Susannah stays in the doorway, biting her nails, looking intensely towards the man riding the horse. Alfred, Tristan's older brother, comes down the stairs in the house, behind Susannah. He has just confessed his love to Susannah in a previous scene; he already feels that she is now his. It's fate. He doesn't know it yet, but his fate is about to change. Alfred is still in his own little world. "I'm going to town," he says. Then, he notices that she's looking at something, transfixed. She hasn't heard him at all. He stands next to her in the doorway and follows her gaze. He sees his brother, Tristan, riding towards the house, backlit by sunlight, a hero coming home. Alfred looks at Susannah, who returns his gaze, says nothing, turns away, and goes into the house. She is already with Tristan. Alfred stares at nothing; it sinks in. He gets it. She loves Tristan. She will never love him. He looks back into the distance with a different look in his eye. This wonderful scene of a homecoming easily sets up the story to come and makes clear everyone's relationship to the returning Tristan.

The timing and direction of this sequence is primarily the work of the director and the DP (director of photography). They have created the architecture of the shots to construct a story and a believable rhythm and time frame within which that story takes place. All of the actors appear to be in the same place within the real time frame of a few minutes. All of the actors appear to be watching the same man, coming from the same place and approaching them at the same pace. In reality, when this sequence was being shot, each group of actors was standing somewhere alone in front of a camera crew and was being told when to look, where to look, when to get up, how many steps to take, when to stop, etc. The actors did not see a man riding in on a horse. They were probably looking at a red flag that was put on a light stand, because that is where the sight line would be if they were looking into the distance at the point where Tristan was riding towards the house. The actors follow the direction and fill in the human emotion to make the scene believable.

In *Legends of the Fall,* the performers were probably all shot around the same set of a ranch in Montana, although they didn't have to be, and the sequence was probably all shot within the same day, although it didn't have to be. It could have been shot on different days in different locations. The shots of Tristan riding towards the house, the ones that everyone is reacting to, were definitely shot on a different day, or at least in a different location. All of the other actors in the scene are either in their trailers keeping warm, or they even could be at home in Los Angeles while a second team is taking all of the different exterior shots of Tristan riding in on a horse. There are a lot of them in this movie, and they were all probably shot at the same time if their seasons were the same. With all of this deconstruction of time and place, actors have to do something to ground themselves to a place and make it look real.

PLACE AS A SENSE MEMORY

Actors create everything out of their own imagination anyway. Everything an actor does is enhanced by his or her imagination, which fills out the moment, hopefully, to its fullest extent. When working with place in film-making, whether in a studio or on a real location, actors have to enhance the situation with their imagination.

As always, there are many approaches to solving the problems presented by place. One of the ways of finding the best methods for you to solve the problems of working with place on a film set is to work on Place as a sense memory. This will help you develop the discipline of creating a 360-degree space around yourself and at the same time develop the emotional control to be connected to the place and given circumstances of the script that you are supposed to be in.

CREATING AN IMAGINARY PLACE

To create an imaginary place, we use the same procedure as creating any of the other sense memories: We begin with the Mental Relaxation exercises and warm up the physical body through movement. In order to create an imaginary place, you have to employ all of your senses and be able to create the space around your entire body. This will not usually come all at once. Sometimes, only a portion of a place will come to you, and for certain circumstances, that will be sufficient.

We have already gone through a "lite" version of creating a place in chapter 2, when I introduced the senses and how they might be used in sense memory. The place we used then was your bedroom. What was missing from that excursion was putting the room further in the past and spending more time with the creation of a 360-degree space.

As with all sense memories, choosing the right ones to work on is very important. I have an exercise that I do with my students to introduce the use of place as a sense memory. When I teach, I normally lead the students through this exercise after they are warmed up. If you are reading this book on your own and want to do this exercise, it's quite possible as well. You will have to make sure that when you decide to do the exercise that you are reading it in an atmosphere of concentrated, undisturbed work. Give yourself at least two hours to start with the Mental Relaxation and then go into the exercise. Read a few steps, and then do them. Then read the next step and do it, and so on and so forth.

THE VACATION EXERCISE

I call this exercise the Vacation exercise, because it begins with your favorite vacation spot from at least seven years ago. The further back you go, the better. When I say favorite vacation, I mean the first memory that comes up in response to the question: What is your favorite vacation spot from at least seven years ago? Whatever memory comes up first, it is the right one and will serve the purpose of the exercise. It doesn't necessarily mean that you had a good time, or that it is indeed your *favorite* vacation—it might have even been a terrible experience—but if it is the first memory that comes up, it's the right one.

1 Lie down on the floor, close your eyes, and allow your mind to wander. Don't be afraid if you feel like you are going to fall asleep. Let yourself go into a sort of dream/awake state. Think of

Creating the Space

the memory of your favorite vacation spot, and allow it to play as a movie in your mind.

2 Start to build the memory through your senses. What were the sights, sounds, smells, tastes, and touches of this experience and place? Ask specific questions, and wait for the answers.

3 When you have reached some fullness of memory, pay more attention to the actual place that you are in, and let go of any scenarios and other people that have entered into the place. Slowly open your eyes, and begin to use your senses to create the space around you. Normally, we would start with sight. If you were lying on the ground in your imaginary place, what would you see if you opened your eyes? Look around you as you try and see the place immediately around you.

4 What would you be lying on in your imaginary place? Sand, grass, a porch? Are you outside?

5 What time of year is it? Ask as many questions as you can think of. Don't worry if you don't get answers. Remember, in many respects there are no answers, just the development of a better question.

6 When you have established some sense of imaginary reality, slowly start to move in the space. Don't get up immediately, always let your movements be led by sensory exploration. For instance, if you are lying in sand, pose the questions: If I am lying in the sand in my memory, what does the sand feel like beneath my body? If I move my hand through the sand, how does it feel between my fingers? What sounds do I hear as I move my body? And so on.

7 As you move through the place exploring your senses, you create the place. Remember, the place is in your imagination. If you stop creating it with your senses, it disappears for the audience. It must exist outside of your self, and that will only happen if you keep exploring it through your senses.

8 Move to a sitting position, and then a standing position if you like. Let your movement be guided by asking sensory questions. Do not get involved in mime-like activities or interacting with imaginary people, etc. You are strictly creating a place around you from your

memory through your senses. Direct the concentration clearly from one thing to the next, systematically.

9 Don't forget to employ all of the relaxation and breathing techniques of the previous chapters to enhance your exploration of the moment.

Once you have created a place around you and you are in the middle of it, you can allow the memories of the place to filter back in. You can employ the Inner Monologue to start to interact with the space. If people figure greatly into your memory, you can speak about them in your Inner Monologue, but you should try to keep from being distracted from creating the place around you. If you allow figures from the past to take over your place sense memory, you may find that it will sabotage and diffuse your concentration. Remember, the primary task is creating the place.

THE STREET WHERE YOU LIVED

We are going to leave the vacation spot now and go to the street where you lived at the time of the vacation. This is not a travel story—one moment you're in the vacation spot, the next you're standing outside the house or apartment building where you lived. Again, the first place that comes up is the right place, even if it isn't correct in terms of the time and space of your life.

1 Notice all aspects of the street where you lived. What time of year is it? Is it consistent with your vacation, or is it a different season and time altogether? Be very careful that you don't direct your memory as if you were making up a story. Let the memory reveal itself to you and lead you down its own path. If you try and make a nice, neat story out of everything, that is to say, make everything coherent and logical, it will be completely useless as an acting tool. You are not creating a little movie in your mind for others to see or to read, you are plowing the fields of your imagination to employ its fruits in someone else's movie. You will use your imagination to flesh out someone else's story.

2 Create the street through your senses as fully as possible. You may want to spend some time on this. Usually, there are many, many memories connected to the places where we live or have lived.

NOTE ABOUT RECALLING MEMORIES: If you find that there aren't any memories or you find yourself becoming bored or tired, it usually means that you are blocked by a major memory that you would prefer not to revisit. To help you overcome this and move forward in the exercise, visualize a chest full of treasures that has one horrible little thing in it, and think of that as your memory bank. Because you don't want to look at or have others *see* this little horrible thing, you never open the chest. You live in poverty, in rags, because your treasure chest has one thing that cannot not be revealed. Strangely enough, if the horrible thing is revealed, everyone else thinks that it's cute, or they have one just like it and they are happy to see another one. Or perhaps they find it fascinating because it is so horrible, and therefore would like to be your friend, so they could learn more about it. In fact, rather than becoming isolated, you gain comrades by exposing your horrible little things.

I am not talking about describing in detail secrets about your past. I am talking about accessing emotions and parts of yourself that will fuel the details of a fictional character. Very often, you have no idea what might constitute your own personal battalion of horrible little things. You only know that you are frozen in some area. Working on Place will often expose these areas of frozen assets. Once they are exposed, what you want to do about them is up to you, depending on the severity of their power over you. If you see that you have a pattern of avoiding certain things or "spacing out" when you encounter certain memories, try the next step.

3 To break this pattern, you should concentrate on a very small corner of your place and attempt to create it through your senses as realistically as possible. Take, for instance, the corner of a stone stoop and the feeling of the cement as your run your finger over the stone. What parts of your body come in contact with the stone if you are sitting there? How many different types of little stones can you see within the cement, or is it smooth? And so on. Stay within a small, very specific portion of the place. Work very small and very exact. Sometimes, this "tricks" the imagination into releasing a much broader bank of memories and objects.

CREATING A ROOM

We are going to change the location again. Go into the house or apartment connected to the street. If it is an apartment building, you may wind up in the hall or stairwell first. That's okay; they're part of your home experience just as much as your apartment. Creating a room is one of the most common usages of the place sense memory.

4 Sit or lie down, and close your eyes. Walk into the house or apartment and look around. As always, use all five senses, and follow the path of the strongest impulses. As you move through the house, come to one room and stay there. Now, start to explore that room. Open your eyes, and begin with what you see. Ask very specific questions. What is the color of the walls? What is on the floor? What is the furniture in this room? What are the objects? When you see something that interests you, reach out your hand and touch it.

5 When you pick up an object, be careful that you are able to stay in the room while you are exploring the object as well. In other words, don't drop the room to investigate an imaginary object. This is difficult to do, but try. It requires discipline and systematic direction of the concentration to keep checking that the room is still there. All of this work should be done in a relaxed manner, allowing the breath to fill out the moments and the Inner Monologue to express the thoughts and feelings of those moments.

6 When you find one segment of the room that is very strong for you and ignites your imagination, stay there, and investigate it more thoroughly. Take time with the small details of patterns on a pillow or the intricacies of a needlepoint that hangs on the wall.

7 Stay in this segment of the room, and create the rest of the room from there. Think of your imagination as concentric circles. You are in the center, at the bull's eye, and the space around you emanates from you. Your imagination is directed by your concentration, and you project it ever farther away from yourself. It's easiest to start small and then work your way to larger and larger spaces. Direct the concentration from the circles closest to you to the circles farthest away and back to the closest again.

BEING THE CHARACTER IN THE ROOM

At this point, it's interesting to bring a character into the play of your imaginary field. This could be any character that you are working on at the moment, but the best one to choose if you are just starting out in this work is the same one from chapter 3 and the Monologue exercise.

The character is introduced like it was just dropped in by parachute. There should be no adjustment of who you are, what you're doing, or your thought patterns. The character is just another loaded parcel of information that you introduce into what is already happening. One nanosecond, you're standing in the living room of the house you grew up in, and the next nanosecond, you're the character in a living room. The only thing you adjust is the life history. Instead of yours, you have your character's. Therefore, you also have your character's words. The place, however, looks the same.

Give yourself some time to just look around the room again as your character. Revisit sensory moments that were strong for you in the room, and see how they have changed now that you've decided that you're the character. Any changes should be very subtle ones. There shouldn't be any evidence of acting at all. Avoid making judgments and decisions about how your character reacts or acts. Just be in the space as the character, and continue the sensorial creation of the imaginary space. When you have adjusted to the way that this feels, begin to say the words of the monologue as if they were your own thoughts. Give the creation of the sensory world the priority of importance over the words. Don't allow the words, and your effort to remember them, destroy the imaginary place that you have created. Keep the place going while you say the text, and create a moment-to-moment reality. If you forget the text (and if you are doing the exercise correctly, you probably will), stop speaking and investigate the sensory moment more fully before you try to continue with the text. If you cannot remember all of the text, just repeat the parts that you do remember, over and over again. Don't worry about what you have forgotten, you can always check to see what it was later.

Usually, we forget words when we don't know what they mean in relation to that acting moment. You always have to give yourself a break when you're learning a new exercise. The very fact that you are exploring new territory overtaxes your instrument, therefore, you forget how to do things that you normally do very easily. When you slow down and keep the sensory going in lieu of the text, you slowly build the words into your imaginary reality. You learn how to incorporate another level into your acting. You expand the ability of your concentration to incorporate ever larger spaces filled with more and more complex objects. Eventually, you are able to put all of your inner work together with the words, the given circumstances of the script, and any direction that you might receive.

When you start to build the character, you always go back and read the script. You read the part and let the part lead you to new discoveries about your sense memory, and you let the sense memory lead you to new discoveries about the part. It's very important to keep working to eventually meld you and the character together. You may even forget what the particulars of the sense memories were. You only remember their keys, and you use them when you need them, when you are at sea with the part or need to inject new life into it. It's always helpful to keep a Journal (see page 39) for a part of all your sense memory work and its connective patterns. It can be used for the part that you are working on now, but also for ones that you might build in the future. An actor working in this medium is best armed with his or her own road map to hold the performance together, because so much of film acting is disjointed. It's always best to have your own blueprints that you can build your characters upon.

PLACE AS AN INNER EMOTIONAL STATE

Sometimes, we experience things in life that stay with us for a long time. These things will revisit our consciousness when we least expect it. Great loss requires periods of mourning, just as traumatic events require a period of adjustment and recuperation. The characters that we play also have these events in their lives. Very often, a script will have scenes that are shot in locations of great beauty about a character who is suffering deeply. We, as audience members, are familiar with these scenes. The lovers breaking up on a bridge in Paris, a child alone and hungry on the streets of New York City, a soldier standing over the bloody battlefield with an exquisite sunset in the background—the extraordinary moments of cinema filled with the contrast of human suffering and physical beauty.

There is such a scene in *Legends of the Fall*, shortly after Tristan's homecoming from the war, where he kneels before his brother's grave and cries in agony and remorse over his loss and inability to have saved his brother's life. The location of this grave is a green field overhanging a gorge, with huge mountains looming in the distance. It is a scene of exceptional natural beauty, but Tristan, played by Brad Pitt, is trapped within an internal place of extreme force, the battlefield where his brother lost his life. The exceptional beauty of Tristan's surroundings may comfort him in the following moments, but not until he has thoroughly revisited the battlefield and mourned for his brother's life at his grave. Here, the actor

Creating the Space

91

brings his internal place to the physical surface, interacts with it emotionally, and creates a place around him. We are drawn into his experience through his emotional outpouring, which is so deep-rooted in his experience in a place we cannot see that we use our own imaginations to feel what he feels, and we empathize. He is deeply involved in the innermost concentric circles, very close to the bull's-eye, where we join him by being deeply involved with our own innermost circles. We use our imagination and experience to empathize. In this way, when an actor is the most personally connected to an inner place, he may be most universally understood, because he is being so profoundly human, and that is something everyone can understand.

THE FOURTH WALL

Creating an inner place of such emotional power is a different usage of place than the creation of a communal *fourth wall*, as all of the actors did in the first scene I mentioned at the beginning of this chapter. Those actors all created the illusion of seeing the same scene before them that we were seeing on the picture screen. The fourth wall is the missing wall of the traditional proscenium arch of the theater, through which the audience views the play. Though there have been amazing technological advances since the days of actors standing on gas lit stages in heavy makeup, projecting their voices, and using large gestures to indicate what is going on, one thing for the most part has not changed—we are still looking at the actors through a frame. Although there have been theater productions that have been site-specific or in the round in the attempt to break away from the proscenium arch, for the most part, we are still inside the box. We are still looking into a frame, and the rules that apply to that rectangle still apply to film. As actors, we are still looking out into the imaginary fourth wall. The difference is that in film, the fourth wall is no longer fixed; it could be moving around us all the time. Wherever the camera stands photographing, so stands the fourth wall or the audience. For the actor on a film set, the fourth wall is wherever the director says it is. Sometimes, it is the camera, sometimes it is not. You just create the space around you as you are told. The interesting thing about this is that you never know what it's going to be until you're on the set. You are just expected to be able to create it as they ask for it.

There are two kinds of places that actors concern themselves with on a film set. One is the actual setting of the scene as depicted in the script, and the other is the personal, private place that actors draw from to help them act. The camera can photograph your thoughts and emotions, so the inner place must be as highly developed as the place that you create physically around yourself. To help you to learn to create these two places at the same time, use the following exercise. It is devised to be done with a partner, although it can be done alone as well, but then one wouldn't do the text. If you are working alone, you would only create the place.

ZOO STORY EXERCISE—PLACE

This exercise works your ability to create two types of places at the same time. It should be done with a partner. We'll use the first four pages of Edward Albee's one-act play, *The Zoo Story*. These pages are about the place, Central Park in New York City, and moving around within that space.

It doesn't matter if you are the right type to play either of the parts of Peter or Jerry. It doesn't even matter if you are the right age or sex. The purpose of the exercise is to create the space around you with your partner, as is required by the text and the given circumstances of the play, while at the same time creating your own personal place that grounds you to a sensorial reality that you can work from to build character. Although this is a play for the stage, it's a good script to use for building the place sense memory and the fourth wall at the same time.

1 Read the one act play, *The Zoo Story*, by Edward Albee, and choose a partner to work with.

2 Choose the part for which you are temperamentally more suited. Age, sex, and type don't matter for the purposes of this exercise. I do it with a classroom full of twenty-year-olds of both sexes, pairing them off indiscriminately.

3 Concentrate on the first four pages of the script or thereabout. I end with the lines:

Jerry: And you have children.

Peter: Yes; two.

4 Read the script aloud together, and discuss the scene. Answer the following questions together:

Where are you? Where does the scene take place?

What's the weather?

What time of year is it?

Are there other people around?

What are the sounds?

What are the smells?

When you look around yourselves in 360 degrees, what do you see?

5 Read the script aloud again, and work on testing out the space you've created together. See how it holds up under the demands of the script.

6 Now, take some time for each of you to remember an outdoor place from your past that you know well.

7 Put the two imaginary places together, the one you have created with your partner and the one you see from your memory. For instance, if you have agreed that Fifth Avenue is to your left at 9:00 o'clock then take note of what is in the place from your memory in that spot, and see that when referring to Fifth Avenue. Of course, this will cause, or should cause, some sort of behavior in you, and that behavior would be put on the character. Take your time.

8 Memorize the lines, and do the scene with the main priority given to creating the place. The scene already demands a strong sense of place, so this shouldn't be too difficult.

9 Stop yourself from performing too broadly or running away with the script. Don't give up your personal private space!

Actors in the same scene must be in the same place in order to create the illusion of that place. Each actor comes from a personal private space that he continually creates with his imagination through the five senses. How an actor achieves this private space is unique to each actor. Usually after years of experience, the actor knows his own instrument to such a degree that he will know what works for him. Some actors "see" the place, for some a sound or a certain smell will do it. Some can use a combination of many sensory objects.

When the actor is working (the camera's rolling), he must be actively creating the imaginary objects, otherwise, these disappear. This is not achieved by indicating or remembering what one did before, but by constantly, actively asking questions and searching for the answers with another question. The above exercise is simple enough for you to give yourself the time to create the surroundings while adhering to the given circumstance of the script and the text. I think you will be surprised to see how much of the character can be discovered by concentrating on the active creation of a place through the senses.

ON SELF-INDULGENCE

When you are working with the private elements of your acting technique as we have been doing in these last few chapters, it's very important to steer away from being self-indulgent and self-involved. Although you're using many private aspects of yourself, the work isn't really about you, it's about the script. Many of the exercises are just that, a means to an end. That end is the character within the screenplay. At every step along the way, always refer back to the script. When you are working, everything you do must fly on the wings of the script; to do otherwise is not artistry. As you work, you develop an intuitive use of self that translates into the universal human experience.

If you are teaching a group, then it is your responsibility as a teacher to make sure that your students' work doesn't become too self-indulgent and that they don't start spinning tricks just to please you and their fellow students. When I do an exercise like the *Zoo Story*/Place exercise, I have everyone working at the same time to discourage the tendency to want to perform and entertain. I watch the groups rehearsing and listen to what they are doing. I'll ask questions and guide them to get their imaginations working more fully. I'll even have everyone stay in the spaces that they have been rehearsing in, and we'll go around the class, each pair taking their turn doing the work that they have prepared, while the other groups watch from their various points around the room. This seems to enhance the 360-degree feeling to the pairs and prepares the actors for a film set, where they might very well be surrounded by the crew and the other members of the cast. The classroom is a perfect atmosphere for creating public privacy, since we're all in it together, just like on a film set. As the groups gain more and more confidence in their imaginary reality and the spheres of public privacy surrounding them, I separate the group into audience and performer and have each group go up and present the work that they have done on the scene. For the purpose of creating imaginary reality, I never mind if all they can accomplish is a few minutes of creating the space together and a few lines of the text. I am happier with that than if they sail through the scene and haven't created anything uniquely private at all.

Of course, the arena of a classroom and the arena of the real world are two completely different ball games. As a teacher or as a student, there is no better way to test and further develop what you have learned than by entering into the real world of filmmaking. The next section of this book will attempt to help you cope as an actor, as you begin to make your way into that labyrinth of exciting and variable possibilities.

PART TWO

THE SCRIPT AND CHARACTER DEVELOPMENT

THE AUDITION

The audition—everyone wants one, everyone hates them—is one of the necessary evils of the actor's life and the way we get jobs. No matter where you are in your career as an actor, the audition comes into your life in one form or another. Even stars at the pinnacle of their careers may have to audition for a part that deviates from their public image. They won't be attending a cattle call, but in one form or another, they will have to convince the director that they are right for the part. It might be at dinner at a four-star restaurant, but it's still a form of auditioning.

Most of us in the acting profession have auditions served in much more modest fashion, on a cold platter, and we're lucky if we get a glass of water. Still, everyone wants an audition, because that's how you get the part. Once you have it lined up, and are about to do it, you're terrified that you won't do it well; then, you won't get the job. The reality is, if you aren't what they're looking for, you won't get the job no matter how well your audition goes. Since there is no way to actually tell what they want from you, regardless of what they might say, the situation causes anxiety, distress, and feelings of powerlessness. One of the things you might as well accept from the outset is that in many respects, you have no control over the decisions of people hiring you. All you can do is take care of the things over which you do have control—your acting technique and your professional demeanor. If you take care of those things, then you will have the confidence you need to go through with the experience.

This section of the book is about what to do once you have an audition and how best to use your technique to get the part. It is not about how to go about getting an audition, nor how to build a career in the movie business. There are many books that deal with that subject matter, and much of the information that you find in them is very useful, but they are only tips—tips that aren't of much use if you don't have any idea of a practical acting technique.

THE TYPICAL MOVIE AUDITION

Unlike theatrical auditions, where they normally ask you to prepare two contrasting monologues, the typical movie audition requires an actor to read from the screenplay to a video camera. You're given a few pages from the script where your character appears. These pages are called "sides." Normally, sides are only two pages long, sometimes three, but not more. This is because scenes in movies tend to climax in about three minutes, and the screenplay page equals one minute of screen time. In some cases, the sides can be picked up a few days in advance, which is great, because you can really work on them. However, most of the time, they just tell you to come in a little early, so that you can "look over the sides before your audition." The person arranging the audition tells you a few key character-istics and a little bit of background about the character when she makes your appointment. "Can you come in on Thursday at 11:00 for the role of Sadie? She's a vampire who doubles as a baby sitter. It's a support-ing role, two days shooting. She looks seventeen, but in reality she's two hundred, so she's very savvy, very smart. She's got a great sexy argument with the husband. Just get there at 10:30 to pick up the sides." And you're off to the races.

You arrive early, pick up the sides, go into the hallway, the stairwell, the bathroom, or if you feel there's enough time, out into the street, read the sides, decide what to do, and go in to take the audition. Sometimes, if the director is there, or the casting agent is sympathetic, you'll receive more information about the part just seconds before you are expected to do it for the camera. You're expected to be flexible and take any adjustment as a compliment that they are interested in what you are doing, but they would just like you to add something else. Always keep what you have going for you and add what they have suggested. Never let an adjustment throw you into believing that everything you have chosen is wrong; just permit their adjustment to affect your work.

SLATING

When it's your turn to audition, you'll go into a small room (usually, they're rather small), meet the casting people, and the director if he or she is there. A brief exchange may follow, but not always. Then you are instructed to either stand or sit on a mark and "slate" before you begin doing the scene. Slating is merely stating your name, agent affiliation, and sometimes social security number. You always slate before a videotaped audition; it's how they identify who you are on the tape. These auditions are videotaped back-to-back and more than likely viewed in the fast forward mode until the director sees something interesting, or rather something that piques his interest, and only then does he play the tape at normal speed and listen to the actor. Long, drawn-out pauses where nothing is happening are not suggested. Each moment has to be used to its fullest potential, so start being the character as soon as you are in front of the camera, even while slating; just take a beat before you begin speaking the lines.

THE READER

There is an assistant in the room, who is the reader. Readers do just that, they read the other character's lines in the scene. You are instructed where to direct your eyes. Sometimes it's to the reader, sometimes to the camera, and sometimes just into space, with the reader's voice coming from one direction and the camera lens photographing you from another. Sometimes, the reader is an actor, and he will actually play the scene with you. It's more likely that the reader is not an actor and will dryly read the other character's lines to you, more as a necessary courtesy than anything else. You simply adjust to the situation; take in the information and instantaneously adjust. You never address the reader other than a simple introduction; you never direct him or request anything from him. Readers are there as administrative assistants, not as acting partners.

TIME

The concept of time is a very strange thing in filmmaking. It's always, hurry up and wait. They need you immediately, you must hurry, hurry, hurry, and then you sit and wait for three hours; no one is able tell you why. Then suddenly you're called to the set (usually just as you've relaxed enough to doze off), and in minutes you're in front of the camera. You're at the center of a buzzing hive of activity, somewhat dazed and confused after hours of inertia.

It can be the same at a film audition. They give you an appointed time for your audition, little time to prepare anything substantial, minimal information, plus stressed-out working conditions. Then you arrive, ready to go, only to find out that you may have to wait an hour or more until they are ready for you. Although they try to keep things running smoothly and on schedule, things don't always work out that way. So, you may arrive an hour before your audition, prepare what you can quickly, and then find out that they're running late and they can't tell you how long it's going to be. You wind up sitting in a cramped office with other actors who are just as anxious as you are and want to dispel their nervousness through idle chatter. You can't leave, because you're afraid to miss your turn, and you aren't able to continue working under the circumstances. This can be a very frustrating work environment, but there's nothing you can do about it except relax and trust in the choices you've already made. You'll have to put all your acting juices on the back burner until it's time to go in. If you stress out and keep going over things again and again in your mind, you will probably be too frazzled to do your best once you get in the room. It's good practice to learn how to gauge yourself under these circumstances, because it's the normal atmosphere of even the most well-organized and smoothly run of film sets. You have to prepare your body, mind, and spirit before you get there.

Auditions are usually scheduled ten minutes apart, so your actual time with the auditioners is probably five to seven minutes max. That's all the time you have to convince them that you're the right one for the part, at least enough to get a callback. All they are looking for at this first round is: what do you look like, what do you sound like, and do you bring reality to the moments of the script that they have given you. You are not responsible for bringing reality to every moment, but you must be able to illuminate something; some aspect of the character must be brought to life in those few minutes. It's useful to know that what you look like accounts for about 75 percent of their decision initially, but a great audition can often change their minds, or at least they'll remember you for another project. In a movie audition, you are not just auditioning for that role, you are auditioning for other projects that the casting director and the director might do in the future. Sometimes, they will even offer you a different role in the same movie because of what they see in your work.

THE BREAKDOWN SERVICES

The most commonly used method of communicating to agents and managers what actors are needed for which auditions is done through Breakdown Services. The Breakdown Services is an independent company that sends a list of all of the projects that are casting to all agents and managers who pay for the service. This list is sent out Monday through Friday, every week of the year, and includes all branches of the entertainment industry: films, television, commercials, special appearances, and all types of theater. The producers, directors, and casting agents who post the auditions with Breakdown Services can do so free of charge. You must be a franchised agent with the three acting unions, SAG, AEA, and AFTRA, or a manager referred by three franchised agents in order to subscribe to the Breakdown Services. It is illegal for anyone else, including actors, to receive the breakdowns.

A breakdown is the list of characters in a screenplay and their types. This usually includes their age, race, what they look like, ethnicity and personality traits. Sometimes, it includes a brief synopsis of what the character does in the movie, whether it's a lead, supporting, day player, cameo, etc. The agents and managers sign a confidentiality agreement that they will not release the breakdown to actors or other third parties. In other words, actors are only supposed to be told about an audition through an agent or manager who is submitting them for a specific part. The descriptions of the characters are written by any number of people: the casting agent or an assistant, a production assistant working on the project, or for an extra fee, Breakdown Services will do it. Sometimes, the director of a movie will write the breakdown, but rarely. The descriptions vary greatly in their style, accuracy, and content. What this means to the actor is, you really never know how accurate the information that has been filtered down to you is in terms of the director's original view of the character. As an actor going into an audition, you should never worry about whether or not you are right for the part. That is something that the director will decide when he sees your audition. Never make that decision for him or let thoughts about it affect your work.

TYPES

Film breakdowns are filled with stereotypical descriptions that describe the "type." A type is a category that you fit into as an actor and also as a human being. Your looks and your nature determine much of your type. It is possible to change your type, but that usually happens by the normal process of aging and maturity. The sweet young thing will eventually be the doting grandmother if she stays in the business long enough; it's just a simple fact of life. Of course, many actors these days invest in extensive plastic surgery in order to change their types or hang on to ones that are slipping through their fingers. I have nothing to say about that; that is a personal matter. What you look like is vastly more important to an actor in the film industry than it is to a stage actor, it's just the simple truth.

We are all well acquainted with these types—the girl next door, the blonde bombshell, the all-American jock, the wisecracking cop, the nerd, the business executive, the mom, the salt-of-the-earth construction worker, the bad boy, the spinster librarian, etc. All of these are stereotypes in our common collective culture; it's the beginning of easily communicating how the actor is expected to look. Whether or not the characters in the film are stereotypes has nothing to do with the way they are often described in the breakdown. The stereotype is a tool of communication, not an edict for behavior.

The breakdown describes the character so that managers and agents will send the right types of actors to the auditions. However, it's a funny thing about types: Everyone is so sure of what they are that everyone believes that his own opinion is correct, and sometimes the signals get crossed. This happened to me one very hot summer in New York City, when a casting director who was a friend of mine called me and said, "There's an audition I want you to go to. I want you to understand that you're definitely not going to get the part; you're totally the wrong type, but I want you to meet this director anyway. She's just starting out, but this is a very interesting project for PBS about a WPA photographer during the depression. It's a good opportunity for her to get to know you for a future project."

So, off I go to some weird address on Allen Street on the Lower East Side. It's 110 degrees in the shade, and I keep thinking, well, I'll just be charming and relaxed, do what ever she wants me to do, and then go somewhere that's dark and air-conditioned for the rest of the afternoon. (My apartment at the time was not air-conditioned.) I sauntered into the audition, which was in a vacant storefront, and I sort of scoffed at the tense-looking actors waiting in the front room. No one there looked liked me, so I guess the casting director was right; there weren't any parts for me in this project. The director was very nice; I had a great time with the audition; I read from the script and talked about the part. I was humorous and serious at the right moments; my laugh came naturally out of the moment. When I left, I thought, "Gee, too bad there isn't a part for me. I'm the wrong type, I'm not even what she's looking for, and she was still so nice to me. We really got along great."

When I got home, there was a message on my service that I had the lead part in the project if I wanted it. I was shocked. I quickly reviewed the situation in my head. What had happened to make her change her mind? True, I had worn a 1930s dress I had from a second hand store, and I did like the script and gave it my best shot, but I'd done similar things in the past, and it hadn't gotten me the job. What was different about this time? Could it be that I convinced her with my relaxed manner that my type was better than the one she originally wanted? Could be, but not likely. I later found out that what happened was, the casting director had misinterpreted the breakdown. In her mind, it had evoked a picture of someone very different from me, but she had a hunch about the director liking me and sent me anyway. It turns out that the director had someone exactly like me in mind for the part, and she knew it the moment I walked through the door; she told me so later. I didn't think I had any chance of getting the part, so my defenses were down, permitting me to expose myself in a way that I didn't usually do in auditions at that time. It was a valuable lesson for me to learn. Regardless of what you have been told, you never know, you might be exactly what they are looking for. So, just relax as much as you can and be yourself.

DOING THE VIDEOTAPED AUDITION

So, let's take a look at how you can apply the techniques from the previous chapters to a videotaped film audition. I'm not a fan of taping yourself to prepare for an audition. The image that you create inside the frame may have nothing to do with the image that a director would create inside the frame; you have moved your focus from acting to filmmaking. There are better ways to prepare for a videotaped audition than becoming a film director.

Let's assume you have received some information about the character from the casting director, but you won't see the sides until the day of the audition. You have to begin with the information that you have. What is it that instinctually attracts you in the part? Forget about the excitement that you feel about the audition, thinking about what it will be like to see yourself on the screen, how great it will be to tell all your friends that you had an audition, got the part, got great reviews, and won the Academy Award. I'm not kidding. Actors have vivid imaginations, and if that's the track your mind is racing around before an audition, put the brakes on, and concentrate on the matters at hand. Take the elements of the part that attract you the most, from whatever information you have, and go to work.

START AT THE BEGINNING: RELAXATION

Even if you receive the sides a few days before your audition, read them once, and then put them aside. Start at the beginning. Start with relaxation. Go through the Mental Relaxation exercises, and use the Inner Monologue to get everything that might interfere with your concentration out of the way. Before you can choose what elements of the part you can carry with you into an audition, the head and neck have to be freed of tension, and the body must be ready to cooperate with directing all impulses into the expressions of the face and the voice, so that they will read in the confines of a close-up camera frame. Normally, the range of movement that you are allowed will be miniscule, because the camera will photograph you in a medium shot or a close-up.

Always be systematic with your work, and put the time aside to work seriously from the very beginning. You should be able to decipher the difference between how you feel about going to audition and the excitement you get from the actual part. You have to find the aspects of the part that generate excitement for you. Even if the character is not necessarily an exciting one, you have to get excited about the challenge of playing it. This excitement must be worked through and not register as nerves in the audition. Just as a singer warms up the voice, the actor warms up the instrument through the relaxation process.

DIRECTING THE FOCUS: CONCENTRATION

The next step will be the concentration. Where will you direct your focus? Your focus cannot be on filming the part; you don't know whether or not you'll get it. You have no control over how the character will look on screen, how it will be photographed, or even, if you should get the part, how much of it will remain in the final edit of the movie, if it appears at all. Don't grant your imagination the license to fantasize on these matters. Instead, focus your imagination on yourself and those elements of yourself that have to do with this part.

You only need one or two elements that you can easily display in the part. Basic truths that apply to the human condition are best. Ask yourself, what is the basic predicament of the character? Is she frightened? Does she feel trapped? Is she in love for the first time? Does she feel powerful? Is she in control? Find a time in your own life that correlates to this condition. It doesn't have to be the exact circumstance, but we have all been frightened, felt trapped, and been in love. It's just a starting point to put you humanly in the same ballpark as your character, playing the same game. It takes a type of self-awareness to do this successfully. The observations and discoveries of the Observation Exercise can help you to develop this skill.

Treat the character as if it were a real person, and draw from your own experience in life. Since you don't know the whole story, you are free to make up your own. You are expected to use your imagination to create a viable human being that looks and talks like you, just with a different history. Don't condemn your character to stereotypical behavior.

Since most movie scripts are fairly simple verbally, the auditioners expect that, given time with the script, you will be able to memorize the lines. They don't expect you to do that if you've only just got them a half an hour before.

Once you have personalized the character, choose the sensory elements that you can construct to display those aspects of yourself that you would like to highlight in the audition. Be aware of the sensual elements of the character and the environment. The use of the sense memories, like Place or Overall, can be particularly helpful. Give your imagination a chance to instruct you how you might best put sensory objects together to create some aspect of the character. Make strong choices. I think it's best for an actor to exhibit the ability to make a choice and follow it through. That's always interesting to watch. If it's the wrong choice, it can be changed later.

Screen characters are evolving all the time; they are being created as you speak. In most cases, they have never existed before. You are creating a new character, and many times, the character is continually evolving even while you are shooting. Sure, there are directors who have a very concrete idea of what they want from the very beginning and aren't willing to deviate from that vision, but I think most are very flexible and rely heavily on an actor's ability to elevate a character into an evolving human being. There's an interview with Martin Sheen in *Hearts of Darkness* where he talks about asking Coppola who his character is, what are his motivations. Sheen says he doesn't understand him and is looking for guidance from his director. Coppola answers him, "He's you, Marty, he's whatever you're feeling and going through at that time. He's you." I think that one of the most exciting aspects of film acting is creating new characters out of the raw material of your own self. You must remain flexible and fluid in your presentation of these ever-evolving characters and be ready to change and add to your character at any time, but the material you draw from is within you.

The sensorial work should be done at home with the information that you have received about the character. Try to find the keys to your sense memories, and test them to see if you can re-create them over and over again if needed. Don't decide how the character acts; avoid preconceived ideas of behavior. Set up your imaginary objects, and interact freely with them. Keep your focus on creating a moment-to-moment imaginary reality.

DEALING WITH THE TEXT

Whether you received the sides a few days in advance or an hour before you walk into your audition, you would deal with them in basically the same way. In the former case, you have more time, and you can be more thorough. In some instances, you might even have received the entire script in advance, which can be as much of a disadvantage as an advantage. There is so much information in a script to choose from that it's very easy to get sidetracked into how you would make this movie, instead of just the small segment of your contribution as the actor. In any case, there are some basic ways of dealing with the sides.

- Read your text, and highlight your lines in a light-colored highlighter. Check the text for all pronunciation problems, verbal difficulties, and definitions of words and places that you need to have clarified. Take care of these things first.

- Make sure that you understand what is going on in the scene from an intellectual point of view.

- Mark all ellipses (a series of periods: …), pauses, and inter-ruptions. You have to know what's happening in those pauses. A series of dots does not mean that you make up the rest of the line. It means that something is happening that is nonverbal.

- Break down the scene into beginning, middle, and end, the same as you would with any script. The basic rules of script analysis apply here as well, generally in a simplified manner.

- Find the beats and transitions—usually there will only be one transition, if any—and take note of them.

- Make note of any questions you have. Be very specific; don't ask something just for the sake of talking.

After you have done these things, speak the text out loud to yourself. If you are in a hallway with other actors, or surrounded by civilians (non-actors), do it any way. You don't have to act it out; just get the words moving in your mouth to find out if there are any pitfalls that you have to fix. If you have already done the preliminary work on the character, your instrument should freely put the text together with any preparations that you have done. The character should start simmering within you, like a slow-cooking stew.

PUTTING THE SCENE IN ITS PROPER PLACE

Every scene has a location where it takes place. If it isn't stated specifically somewhere in the script, it can usually be construed. You're somewhere, and it's not a bad idea to at least give a nod to the place. If you are drinking with a friend in a crowded bar, your behavior is different than if you are whispering to a baby in its crib in the middle of the night. It just makes sense.

You can also create a place while the other character is speaking. Listen to him, but see the place around you. If you have worked on a place for your character, then just take a tiny part of it, like the color of the walls or the way the sunlight would fall into the room at a certain time of day, and lightly direct your focus to create the imaginary objects. A few seconds of truth in creating the environment around you makes all the difference in the world.

Once you have the preparation that you have done at home and the sides of your scene, you must make quick choices of which elements you will actually bring into the audition with you. Unless you are extremely facile in creating an imaginary reality, I would suggest only trying to create some of the place and one other imaginary object in the actual audition. I know it sounds like a lot of balls to juggle, but if you permit your imagination to work freely, then much of what you have worked on previously will fall into place if you remain relaxed by focusing on the moment-to-moment reality within the text. All of the exercises where you are thinking one thing (your Inner Monologue or the writings from your Journal) and speaking another should prepare you to say lines that you have recently received and create the imaginary reality of your character in the scene. You have to trust your work and keep moving forward through the moments. If something doesn't work, you may incorporate its failure into what you are going to do next, if you wish, but don't get hung up on it. Let it go, and move forward.

A trained actor's instrument should work as an integrated being. Everything that you do towards the part affects each step of the work. The text informs the character, just as the sense memory informs the text. Any adjustments from the director inform the whole, and the actor remains relaxed and concentrated as he or she moves forward through the part. You move forward with the actions and needs of the character, just like you would do with any acting script.

DIFFERENT TYPES OF AUDITIONS

The different types of auditions that you might encounter will be determined by where you are in your present career as an actor. Well-known actors usually don't audition for parts; everyone knows their work already. However, if a famous actor is hot to play a part that he is not being considered for, he will often send a professional videotape of himself playing the character. If you are just starting out and have no professional film experience, this course of action is usually a waste of time. You have to accept where you are in the business and try and take the next logical step to advance your career. I once had a friend who was very upset when Madonna got the part of Evita, because she felt that she looked so much more like Eva Peron than Madonna did, therefore, she felt she would be able to play the part so much better. It was true that her resemblance to the real Eva Peron was uncanny, but she had never made a movie and had only just begun to take acting lessons! For her to even engage in such thoughts was a waste of time and energy. There are some parts that are out of your reach; they are going to be played by a star, and that's that.

THE INTERVIEW

Some directors will go for the more relaxed European approach to auditioning and start with informal interviews. There's nothing to do but be the best of yourself, with a slight leaning to the parts of your personality that are exhibited in the part. It's very important to be positive and professional in this situation. Filmmaking requires many hours of enforced companionship with the others on the set, so everyone must get along and keep the work atmosphere positive.

If you are a member of the Screen Actors Guild (SAG), you are allowed to interview once without being paid. Theoretically, if they want to start to work with you more—have you audition with memorized text or do scenes with other actors being considered for the cast—they are supposed to pay you for your time. If you are not a member of SAG—and if you are just starting out, you won't be—then, you aren't protected by the union, and you may encounter many different scenarios that are used as a selection process for actors. In fact, because the Screen Actors Guild has expanded its contracts to include many different levels of low-budget films, including student films, even if you are a SAG member, you will encounter different variations on the audition theme if you go up for these lower-budget projects.

I would suggest you use your instincts in these situations. Always check what part of town you are going to and whether it is a private residence or an office. Never do anything that you don't want to do; if you don't want to do what they are asking you to do in an audition, you are not going to want to work with these people anyway. Know your own nature, and stick by your boundaries. Sometimes, with the lower-budget films, the people running the auditions have little experience in the field; they may be just starting out themselves, and they will make mistakes. You must use your judgment in these circumstances—are they just inexperienced but with good intentions, are they totally inept, or are they savvy and trying to take advantage of you? Usually, the audition will be the telltale heart of the way the rest of the project will be run.

You should be proud of being an actor. You should have integrity, and the heritage of actors, both on and off the screen, should give you strength and confidence, two qualities you'll need to land a job. Screen Actors Guild is one of the strongest labor unions in the world, with a great history all its own.

WHAT IS THE SCREEN ACTORS GUILD?

The Screen Actors Guild is a labor union for actors in motion pictures in the United States of America. Its jurisdiction encompasses most films that you see, most of the prime-time dramatic television programs, and most of the television commercials. Through collective bargaining with producers of these films and programs, SAG governs how actors are hired, how they are treated while they are working, and how much they are paid for their services.

All actors working under SAG contracts receive the same minimum payment and the same regulated treatment (overtime, meals, transportation, etc.) without any negotiation. The Guild has already negotiated the terms of the contract for them. Of course, depending on who you are in the profession and your clout, you can always negotiate for better than the minimum terms. Usually, an agent or a lawyer will handle these negotiations. Most actors are working for the minimum, which isn't a bad day's work, when you can get it.

We all hear a lot about how much money movie stars make and how wealthy and glamorous they are; we fuel our dreams with visions of fame and wealth. However, it is important to note that most of the membership of the Screen Actors Guild makes less than $7,500 a year and that at any given time, 80 percent of the membership is unemployed. An actor, therefore, must be very resourceful if he wants to make a living; usually, actors have several sources of income in order to make ends meet between jobs. There's a German phrase, *Lebenskunstler*. Literally translated, it means "an artist of life," and certainly every actor I know is a brilliant *Lebenskunstler*. They have to be able to survive, and they're usually happy and proud of their chosen profession. They have a joy in living that exudes from every pore; it is this quality that sets them apart from the pack and makes them attractive to watch.

When you join the Guild, the following statement is included with your orientation materials: "I understand that obtaining employment in the motion picture industry is my own responsibility and that it is not the function of the Screen Actors Guild to secure employment for its members."

What the Guild does do is enforces its contracts and arbitrates on behalf of any actor who feels that his contract has been violated. The Guild is very powerful because of its strength in numbers, but also because the stars and the very successful actors are diligent union members. They stick by the union, so the unknown and beginning actor has protection as well, sheltered by the wings of the famous. Some very famous actors have been president of the Screen Actors Guild over the years: James Cagney (1942–44),

Ronald Reagan (elected twice: 1947–52 and again from 1959–60), Charleton Heston (1965–71), Ed Asner (1981–85), Patty Duke (1985–88), and Melissa Gilbert began her term in 2002.

SAG has a great history of actors uniting for better working conditions. The Guild was started in 1933 by a small group of very brave actors who decided they could band together against the extremely powerful studios and fight for better working conditions. Back in the thirties, an actor might earn six or eight dollars a day, fifteen dollars for a week. There were no limits on working hours and no safety regulations, so an actor's day might start at 4:30 AM and end at midnight, with no breaks for meals and no place to rest between shots. Actors did what they were told for fear of never working again; there was always another actor eager to take your place.

If you would like to learn more about SAG, its history, what it does, how it operates, and how you become a member, I would suggest you visit SAG's Web page at *www.sag.com*. It's extremely informative.

DO IT AS OFTEN AS YOU CAN

There are so many things that one can say about auditions and how to handle them, but I think the most important advice is to do as many of them as you possibly can. That way, you can develop your own strengths in presenting yourself; experience is the best teacher in this matter. There are many aspects of yourself that will only come to light in practice; they cannot be guessed at or assumed beforehand. Just as I would suggest not to prejudge your character's behavior, I would suggest not to prejudge your own behavior under the pressure of auditioning. You never know how any given situation will make you react, and often, your own assessment of the situation will be incorrect. So, don't be harsh on yourself; just keep auditioning.

The next chapter will deal with how to prepare a character for the film shoot once you have gotten the part and the script.

READING THE SCRIPT

It's great to be an actor with a good role in a movie, script in hand, and ready to get to work on the character. What's the first thing you're looking for when you open the script and begin to read? Are you looking for the dramatic scope of the character, the wonderful lines that you will speak, or the great scenes that you'll get to play? Perhaps, but speaking for myself, I know the first question I want to answer—how big is my role? I want to know how many times my character appears in the script and what are the locations of those appearances. I want to know how my character is described and with whom she interacts.

I have this technique of quickly breezing through the pages and noting with a Post-it the scenes that include my character. Then I will start at the beginning, reading only the scenes that I have marked, to get a picture of this character as she stands by herself. I ask myself, what kind of life does this character lead as she is represented in the screenplay, and what is happening to her in the moments not shown in the script? I also ask myself whether or not I am interested in doing the part at all. Sometimes we work because we have to, and if I find that I am not interested in the part, I quickly reprogram my thought process for reversal and decide to love her anyway. If I don't love my character I can't work on her, so I've got to find a way to bring her into my heart. I have always been able to find a way to love her.

Then I'll start at the beginning of the script and read the screenplay straight through. As I read, I see the movie and I see myself as a part of it. If the screenplay does not evoke images, it is not a good screenplay. The script of a movie should tell you what you see and what you hear; if it does not do this, then it has failed. The script should flow evenly from one scene to another, without any confusion on the part of the reader; reading it should be easy.

The screenplay format gives everyone on the cast and crew the information that they will need to begin doing their jobs. It's the same with the actor. Most actors will go straight for the dialogue in a script and want to know what they have to say. This is a mistake, because dialogue is the thing most likely to change in a film. This is partially because it is the easiest and the cheapest thing to change, but also because movies are about pictures, not words; the words will be altered to fit the visual construct of the movie. It's more important to take a good look at *where* and *when* your character appears and *what* the character does in any given circumstance. We have to look at the actions; they will tell us who the character is. What she says is just the icing on the cake.

IMPORTANT ELEMENTS OF SCREENPLAY FORMAT FOR THE ACTOR

A screenplay is an ever-evolving written form that changes many times in its life. The first form that could possibly come into the actor's hands is a spec script. A spec script is what writers use as a selling tool to agents, producers, star actors, directors, etc., anyone who will possibly be influential in buying the script and making the movie. Directors who write their own material also do spec scripts because they are easier to read and include much descriptive information that will be excluded from the production or shooting script.

A spec script is more about the story and the actors; a shooting script is more about the visuals and the camera. The shooting script will have scene numbers, camera angles and what we see; it will have less description of the characters. A shooting script usually has less dialogue as well; there is no need to repeat in words what has already been made clear in pictures. Once a director has started to visualize the story, his vision will be incorporated into the wording of all the elements of the script. The script gives you the characters, dialogue, plot, and structure, and the director decides how to put them on the screen. So let's take a look at the elements of the screenplay format and what they mean to the actor.

SCENE SLUGS

A scene slug is one line in caps that describes the location of the scene. It has three essential elements:

1. The location type—this tells us whether we are inside or outside. **INT**. for an interior, **EXT**. for an exterior location. Interior is inside of something—a room, a car, a ship, a hallway. An exterior is in the open air—on a street, in a meadow, on a rooftop, the back of a pickup truck. Special effects make it possible to have exterior locations in a studio, but that probably will not be noted in the screenplay; that information will come to you through the production staff.

2. The location description—a brief description of the place. For example:

INT. ALINA'S APARTMENT

The scene that follows this slug will take place in either a real apartment or in a set built in a studio (or a studio-type setting, like a warehouse) that will look like the inside of an apartment. In either case, you will be inside.

INT. JOE'S BAR

The same is true for this slug, except the location will be a bar, either a real one or a studio set. The nice thing about shooting in a studio set is that it is constructed for the needs of filmmaking—the ceilings are high, with plenty of space for hanging lights, and the walls move for the various needs of the camera. Shoots always go faster in a studio setting than in a real place. Real places constrict the movements of the crew and equipment, which causes everything to move much more slowly.

EXT. TIMES SQUARE

The scene following this slug will be outside on a street, either the real Times Square in New York City or some other street that is going to double for Times Square. You will be outside on the street in either case.

EXT. BEACH

This is very simply outdoors on a beach. Shooting in a barren location like a beach can be very challenging, because you are at the mercy of the weather, and as we all know, that can be very unpredictable.

The description always goes from the general to the specific.

INT. ALINA'S APARTMENT — KITCHEN

This location will be inside the apartment, and the scene will take place in the kitchen. In filmmaking, it is quite possible to have the living room of Alina's apartment in a rented real apartment in New Jersey and the kitchen built in a studio in Los Angeles. It's also possible that the kitchen is the only room that exists in this apartment because it is the only room that appears in the screen-play.

3. The time of day—this is limited to DAY or NIGHT. If the actual time of day is absolutely necessary to the plot it will be included. Mostly it is left out.

INT. ALINA'S APARTMENT — KITCHEN — DAY

Here we are in Alina's apartment, in the kitchen, and it's daytime. However, since we are inside it could actually be any time of day, because the light will be artificially created anyway. If it is an exterior location (EXT.), then it would have to be the time of day that the slug suggests. This is particularly important to note if there are a lot of exterior night scenes in the script. Exterior night shoots, especially in the colder months, can be brutal.

If the date is important, it will be included in parentheses.

INT. ALINA'S APARTMENT — KITCHEN — DAY (1950)

This scene will take place in the year 1950, and every effort that the budget permits will be made to create the look of that era. That includes dressing the actors in the clothes, makeup, and hairstyles of that era. This could mean quite a lot to actors, depending on the fashions of the day. Some fashions could require a long preparation and greatly affect your mannerisms and movement. It's always a good idea to do some research into the current events and fashions of the time that is depicted in the script, because this knowledge can greatly inform your portrayal of the character.

If the scene is a flashback, dream sequence, or projection to the future, it will also be included in parentheses.

**INT. ALINA'S APARTMENT — KITCHEN — DAY
(1950) (FLASHBACK)**

This scene slug tells you that most of the narrative takes place in the present day, but this particular scene is a flashback to the year 1950. It might be a character's memory or a storytelling device to inform the audience of something that occurred in the past that affects the present-day plot. If Alina's kitchen appears in the present-day portion of the script as well as in a flashback sequence, the art department will have to re-dress the present-day set for 1950. What this means to the actor is that all the present-day scenes will be shot in succession, you will shoot somewhere else while the set is being dressed, and then all the flashback scenes at this location will be shot in succession. This will occur regardless of the order in which these scenes appear in the script.

**EXT. TIMES SQUARE — NIGHT (1944)
(DREAM SEQUENCE)**

Well, a dream sequence is anybody's guess because it is so subjective. Be prepared for anything. How this will appear as a dream can only be conveyed by discussions with the director or assistant director. It is possible that the camera and special effects make it look like a dream, or it could be conveyed by the actor's interpretation of the scene. In either case, the sky's the limit.

When the sequence is over it is also noted in the slug. Sometimes the next scene is not in the same location in the script, but it still will be noted that the scene is occurring in the present, whatever the present of that particular film is.

**INT. ALINA'S APARTMENT — KITCHEN — DAY
(BACK TO PRESENT)
or
EXT. TIMES SQUARE — NIGHT (PRESENT DAY)**

The slug line places the scene in time and space. If you can read the slug lines correctly and understand how much information is in them for you, you can start building your character by constructing the world that she lives in; the world that she frequents in the film.

If you are a day player, in one scene, in one location, then time and place aren't so much of a problem. But if you are a lead or supporting character, who appears many different times throughout the movie, it is absolutely necessary to pay close attention to your scene slugs. Actors who know how to carry a movie have paid close attention to the information given to them in the slugs of a screenplay and they are prepared for each and every one of them.

When you are reading a screenplay it should flow from one location and time period to another. There should never be any confusion about where and when a scene is taking place and who the characters in it are. Each new location is given a slug line. If you are moving from room to room in the same apartment, each room has a new slug line.

DESCRIPTION: COPY BLOCKS

Active descriptive copy, written in the present tense, describing what is taking place always follows a slug line; it never stands alone. A slug line tells you where and when; the description tells you what you see and what you hear. Those are the two senses that dominate in films because those sensorial experiences can be directly communicated to an audience—sight and sound.

Copy blocks do not include subtext; that is the job of the actor and director. Subtext is conveyed through the visual impact of the pictures that make up the movie and the performers' inner life. Example:

INT. ALINA'S APARTMENT — KITCHEN — DAY
Alina cooks at the stove. She listens to a Lithuanian program on an AM radio station.

If you are playing Alina, you will be standing in your kitchen cooking, or pretending to cook, depending on the shot. More than likely there will be no radio program playing; the sound track will be laid down in postproduction. What this moment reveals about your character is a point of discussion with your director. If the director has no opinion on it, which is often the case, or asks you what your opinion is, then you should use the scene to reveal something about the character. The actor is often free to make sensorial choices that will enlighten an aspect of the character whom she is playing. For instance, in this case you are listening to something; it is your choice completely what you are listening to and how or if it affects you. Whatever you choose to create is part of your imaginary reality as an actor and should move the character forward in the life of the script.

Moving pictures are very powerful images that shouldn't be wasted; always make a choice for every moment that your character appears. Make a choice about revealing a private moment in a person's (your character's) life. Making a choice in this case doesn't mean making an ironclad decision. It just means that you have thought about it in your preparation, at least enough to have an opinion and something that you could bring to the moment.

Many sounds that are heard in a description are written in caps.

EXT. TIMES SQUARE — NIGHT
Joe walks down the street. He stops to look at the movie marquee. He takes out his cigarettes and smokes. He hears a GUNSHOT.

If we assume that character is shown through action, we will have to develop our characters from the descriptions that follow the slugs. These descriptions clue you in to which imaginary realities you will have to create while performing what actions. In the above example of Times Square, the actor will have to create place, even though the scene will be shot on location. If the director wants to do close-ups on you, and every actor hopes that will be the case, you will need to create something that you're looking at when the camera's lens is in your line of vision. It is very risky to rely on a location to give you reality, you should always be prepared with imaginary objects that are like the actual place that you are in, but with which you have a personal, parallel relationship.

Let's say you happen to have a personal relationship with Times Square; then you must make your imaginary work very specific. Choose a place in time and a particular event, and work on it during your preparation. Select keys from this exercise that you can carry with you onto a set and re-create if needed. Remember, the key must be a sensorial element. It must be light and easy to control, and it must occur in the senses in order to transfer successfully to the character; it cannot be just a thought. To *think* about something, that is to say, to have a mental image to create a sense of reality while acting, only serves to place you in your head, make you tense, and cut you off from your surroundings. This disconnects the actor from the character and the story. Depending on the nature of the thoughts, it can also become extremely self-indulgent. The thought that registers best on the screen is the thought process that is the natural reaction to sensorial response, not an intellectual process of reminiscence.

The actor playing Joe will also have to create the sound of the gunshot and his reaction to it. The description tells you that the audience sees Joe as he hears the gunshot. That means the audience experiences the meaning of the gunshot as it is relative to Joe and his predicament. That can require a lot of preparation work on the part of the actor, depending on the particulars of the script and what the director has explained.

Most people, I would presume, have never heard a gun go off on a busy city street, so the actor must give consideration to the "what if's" of the situation and find a response grounded in his own life that is *like* the one in the film. "What if's" are a series of questions that you ask yourself that begin with the words "what if." It is similar to the questions that one asks oneself while assessing the exercises of the previous chapters, only now you place yourself in the center of a dramatic moment and pose the question as if the event were happening to you. The answers come from the knowledge that you have garnered from frequent self-observation and intuitive knowledge of self. The questions you pose to yourself are formulated from the given circumstances of the script:

What if I knew someone was trying to kill me and I heard a gunshot while I was walking down the street? How would I react?

What if I heard a gunshot and it shocked me so that I couldn't move out of harm's way? How would I react?

What if I got shot and was killed or badly injured? How would I react? Where did the bullet enter? What are the clinical realities of such a wound?

What if I was erroneously accused of a crime? How would I react?

And so forth.

You always start with how *you* would react to a given circumstance, then move to the character's needs. Starting with yourself puts you in the human arena. If you feel that your character reacts differently than you would, you must identify the cause on an experiential plane and implement that difference in the form of sensual reality. If you don't do this the character's reactions remain ideas, and they will render themselves thin and false on the screen. Again, it takes a highly developed sense of observation and a keen sense of focus and concentration to accomplish this successfully.

A problem that occurs with young actors today is that they have seen a lot of movies in their lives, and they observe those movies to see how to act and react to given circumstances. This creates a watered-down, shallow version of human behavior. It becomes a parody, an impersonation of life, rather than an honest observation of oneself and the surrounding world. When acting for the camera you must be yourself even in imaginary circumstances. Since any given scene may have a various number of takes, it is possible to offer multiple interpretations of a reaction from which the director can choose when editing. The beauty of filmmaking is the freedom of the choice. If the budget and your relationship with the director permits, you can always ask to try something for an alternate editing choice if you feel the need to do so. Most directors are happy to oblige if there is time.

CHARACTER INTRODUCTION

When a character is mentioned for the first time in a screenplay, the name appears in caps and is followed by a brief description. If the character of Alina was being introduced for the first time, it might read something like this:

INT. ALINA'S APARTMENT — KITCHEN — DAY
ALINA, a sturdy grandmother with a weathered face, cooks at the stove. She listens to a Lithuanian program on an AM radio station.

Every time the character's name appears after the introduction, it appears in normal upper and lower case spelling: Alina.

Characters that supply only a function are called by that function, even if they have lines and are important to the plot, for example: WAITRESS, POLICEMAN, DRUNK, etc. If there is more than one drunk in the script, they will be DRUNK #1, DRUNK #2, DRUNK #3, and so on. Example:

EXT. TIMES SQUARE — NIGHT
Joe walks down the street. He stops to look at the movie marquee. He takes out his cigarettes and smokes. He hears a GUNSHOT.

```
Two POLICEMEN run toward the movie theater with their
guns drawn.
```

POLICEMAN #1

```
Everybody clear this entranceway! NOW!
```

POLICEMAN #2

```
Move it, people! C'mon, let's go! Get a move on!
```

Roles like Policeman #1 and Policeman #2 can be a lot of fun to play because you, the actor, are often given free reign to create an entire character from whatever small morsels the script has handed to you. Usually the interpretation that you make at the audition is the interpretation that they want you to do on the set. If you were hired for the part, they want you and whatever it is that you did at your audition to show up when the camera is rolling. You will be expected to offer a strong, complete character without any discussion about it. Actors are expected to make strong character choices on their own, and often, directors will only speak to you if you are doing something that displeases them. It is quite possible to work on a movie and never meet the director, except for a brief introduction. You get all your information from an assistant director or from a production assistant, who gives you blocking and logistical notes.

DIALOGUE

A character's dialogue is marked by a centered character slug (the name of the character written in caps) with the dialogue that is to be spoken by that character directly beneath it.

JOE

```
Hey, Aggie, gimme a cuppa coffee and a toasted
bialy to go.
```

AGGIE

```
Cream 'n'sugar, butter on the bialy?
```

JOE

```
Milk, if ya' don't mind, and a smear.
```

Dialogue is almost exclusively in the context of a scene, taking place in an active state and spoken to other cast members. It is rarely spoken directly to the camera and the audience. The illusion of a parallel-enclosed reality on the screen is strictly enforced. When a direction or action is needed, it is included in a parenthetical directly underneath the character slug or interspersed between the dialogue.

JOE
(yells above the din)
Hey, Aggie, gimme a cuppa coffee and a toasted bialy
to go.

AGGIE
Cream 'n' sugar, butter on the bialy?

JOE
Milk, if ya' don't mind...
(sees something out the window)
...and a smear.

Here we know that Joe is speaking in a loud voice and that he sees something outside, through the window of the coffee shop, that catches his attention. Again the particulars of the script will tell you what the nature of this reaction will be, but, as in the case of the gunshot, Joe has to be prepared to create an isolated reaction shot separately for the camera.

The ellipsis marks (a series of three dots) means there is a nonverbal action that takes place in that spot; it does not mean that you should ad lib the rest of the line. In the above example, you have been told exactly what is happening. Many times a direction is omitted, in which case the action is often of an emotional nature.

ALINA
I'm so sorry...I didn't mean to...hurt your feelings....

The ellipsis marks in the above example signify a pause in speaking, in which something nonverbal is happening. It isn't necessarily indecision or hesitation; the choice is open to an actor's interpretation. Directors don't care for parenthetical directions in scripts much, they prefer to give direction on the set based on what is happening in the moment, but if they are left in, then it means that the direction should be taken.

ALINA

(bursts into tears)

I'm so sorry...I didn't mean to...hurt your feelings....

The parenthetical in this case must be executed in a fashion that will read as real emotion for the camera. If the director wants a certain type of tear flowing down the cheek for a certain look and you are not able to produce it satisfactorily, there are always synthetic tears. However, it is assumed that behind the synthetic tears, the actress playing Alina can produce the underpinnings of true emotion that will be humanly appropriate for this particular dramatic moment. The actress is expected to be able to manufacture the necessary emotion on cue, without help from the director. Many actors pride themselves in never having to use synthetic tears. I personally think that a combination of the real ones and the fake ones makes for the best results in many instances.

People erroneously think that a great director pulls the performances out of actors and shows them the way to all this emotion. A great director *chooses* the right actors for the job; actors who know their own emotional landscape and are ready, willing, and able to create whatever is necessary for the picture. The director supplies the space, a few words of encouragement, and the guidance of showing you his vision of the project. Actors know what they have to do to produce that vision on their own.

APPROACHING THE TEXT

So, what about the dialogue for a movie role? What's the best way to approach it? The approach to memorizing text in a film is quite different from memorizing text for a theatrical performance. In theater there are rehearsals; the director and the actors meet one another and talk. The play is worked on bit by bit, until it exists as a whole in a continuous fashion that makes sense to everyone involved, or at least that's the general goal.

Not so with a movie. Many times, there are no rehearsals at all, except for a brief run-through of the text on the set right before you shoot the scene. Often, you haven't met your fellow actors until you are in Makeup and Wardrobe on the day of the shoot; many times you meet them on the set right before you are ready to shoot the scene. Sometimes you don't even meet the director until you are ready to shoot. The script may have changed many times since you last saw it, and it might change again before you're done with the day's shooting. One thing that is not likely to change is the action and what the scene is about. Each scene in a movie is like a building block, and its internal structure within the whole stays pretty much the same.

Directors are usually willing to change the text if it's too stilted or isn't working for the scene and the actors sound stiff. They may simply say, "Let's fix this," and pull out a pen and start crossing out and adding as they go. The actor is usually part of this process, and good film actors will naturally change text to make it more suitable for the action of the moment. I know every auteur director and screenwriter is cringing in their seats after reading this and saying to themselves, "Not with my script, not with my words," but in reality there are very few screenplays that are so perfect that they can't be improved when the actors enter the set to shoot the scene. Many experienced directors will talk about how all the preparation and vision in the world are only the beginning foundations that they build upon. When the actors come onto the set, there has to be flexibility for spontaneous creativity to take place for the betterment of the whole. This process often includes changing the text.

Certainly the dialogue must be worked on; all problems you might have in executing it have to be solved before you get to the set. It must be perfectly memorized. I know all the stories about actors in movies not knowing their lines, but that is a misrepresentation of the truth. *Movie actors are expected to know their lines perfectly without any rehearsal at all.* They must be quick studies who are able to completely change their interpretation at a moment's notice, as well as being totally comfortable with line changes, sometimes significant ones, that are instantly incorporated into the performance that is in the process of being shot. Flexibility is the key word here.

Every actor learns from experience what method of memorizing works best for her under these circumstances. I would suggest learning your lines devoid of emotion, with someone else holding book and reading all the other parts. You should be able to pick up your cues like you would in a speed-through rehearsal. It's also helpful if you can do something else while you say the lines, something mindless like doing the dishes or cooking.

ON THE SET

When I was working on *Another 48 Hrs.*, I had a long scene with Nick Nolte in a bar. My dialogue contained a lot of important information to set up some of the action for the rest of the movie. The day before we were to shoot this scene, the director, Walter Hill, sent me home early to work on my lines and get ready for the scene. We were going to start with that scene first thing in the morning. That would mean rising at 5:00 AM, being picked up at 5:30, hair and makeup at 6:00. I met Nick Nolte for the first time when he came into the makeup trailer at 7:00 AM. The makeup supervisor introduced us, and we chatted briefly. It was very pleasant, and we liked one another. At 9:00 AM sharp we were on the set: Nick Nolte, me, the director, the crew, a rock band on the stage, and two hundred extras dressed for a Saturday night out in a jumping West Coast bar.

Walter places us on the set, the cameras and lights have only a few adjustments before they are ready to go, and Walter says, "Let's run the lines." So Nick and I do the scene. Word perfect, first try. We both know what the scene is about without having discussed it, we both know our lines, and we just jump in. Walter says, "Great, now let's fix this." Out comes his pencil, he looks at me—the least experienced in the group, but I have the opening line—and he says, "What's wrong with this line? It sounds funny. Can you change it?" I have a suggestion and in a few seconds Nick, Walter, and I have our heads together, leaning over the fake bar, and we're working on the script—crossing out and adding words, saying, "What about if I say this, and then . . . ," and we change all the connecting sentences. The scene is essentially the same, the information is the same, but it flows more naturally, like it would between the two characters we were playing, the bartender and an interrogating cop, in loud bar on a Saturday night. The script girl makes all the necessary changes in her log, and it becomes the dialogue in the movie.

FOLLOWING THE BLUEPRINT

A screenplay is a blueprint for an actor's preparation. It only gives you the bare bones, the outer shell, but that's all you need to fire your imagination and begin to technically create the character. Filmmaking is a collaborative art, where everyone does his job separately and thoroughly, then works collectively under the aegis of the director, who shows everyone the way to collaboratively put it all together. Somehow, because only the bare bones are given to you and you are only one part of a greater whole, you have a tremendous amount of freedom for interpretation and insight. Your personal input is essential.

Although the actual mechanics of shooting a film can feel very constricting, I think actors should feel free to exercise their imaginations and personalities to the fullest extent that their talent deems possible. Understanding the structure of the format, and continuing to comprehend the language of film, will increase your freedom with each new bit of knowledge that you gain.

The next chapter will help you to create a structure for your own preparation of a film role. This way whatever time you have to prepare can be used to the fullest extent, and whatever discoveries you have made during this preparation time will be at your fingertips during shooting.

CREATING THE CHARACTER

Everyone has her own method of creating a character. Each actor develops a unique approach that works for her. Whatever your method, there are some elements that should remain universal to all approaches. Preparation work should always be preceded by some form of relaxation. Relaxation is a step that cannot be excluded; whether you have a few months to prepare a role or a few minutes to make a choice, the process should always begin with relaxation.

Tension, undiscovered and unreleased, will only cramp your impulse and cloud your judgment. Sometimes all it takes is one breath and a second of concentration to investigate the tension and relinquish the impulse in the tension's release. Regardless of the amount of time that you have to prepare—and sometimes, it's precious little time—the relaxation process must be incorporated into every new choice. A systematic method of investigating the tension, finding it, and releasing it into the impulse will always yield a choice that can be used, either as it is offered to the director or changed through his direction.

Here are some suggestions that I have used for character preparation while in the process of shooting a film. This framework can be used for any character but is of particular use if you are playing a lead or supporting role that will occur throughout a film. I hope that you can take away some of my suggestions and develop them in ways that work for you.

LOCATION, LOCATION, LOCATION

Movies are planned and shot around the availability of their locations, rather than in the order of the sequence of events as they occur in the screenplay. Most of the time, all scenes that take place in a given location will be shot on that location sequentially, regardless of their placement in the screenplay. For example, if the movie is centered around an interior location of an apartment where the main characters live, and there are many different exterior scenes that these characters go to throughout the movie, then all the apartment scenes will be shot in sequence, and the exterior shots will be shot when their locations can be secured.

A "secured location" is one that has been confirmed for the film crew to come in and shoot, with all necessary permits and equipment in order, for a particular date and time. Exterior locations are always subject to weather conditions and other unpredictable circumstances, so a location shooting date may change often and easily. It is not uncommon for you to show up one day expecting that one scene will be shot, only to find out that for unforeseen reasons that location could not be secured for that day and you will be shooting a completely different scene.

A famous actor's schedule may be taken into consideration when planning a production, but this can only be done to a certain extent. It's only the bigger-budget movies that can afford a big name actor to begin with, and furthermore, to wait for that actor to become available. Most productions do not have that privilege. Location and the technical needs of the script will reign supreme when planning a movie's shooting schedule. The actor's performance is rarely considered, simply because the actor, a human being, can be reasoned with, directed, cajoled, and convinced. This is not the case with camera equipment or the weather.

Everyone involved would like to start somewhere near the beginning of the script and work his way through to the end as much as possible. And it's certainly true that no one is interested in sabotaging an actor's performance, but the simple fact remains that films are expensive to make, and the technical needs of the picture take precedence over the actor's needs. No matter how wonderful an actor's performance is, if it is not photographed correctly and captured on film, it will not be seen. Therefore, the technical requirements and locations reign supreme in planning a filming schedule.

Actors need to realize what they are up against when making a film and take these priorities into consideration when preparing the character.

CHARACTER'S LOG

In order to prepare for the disjointed succession of time in a shooting schedule, I suggest making a special log of your character's scenes in the order that they appear in the script. I would suggest using:

- A loose-leaf notebook, to add and subtract pages as needed.

- Scenes listed by number and slug line, in the order they appear in the script.

- Tabs to separate and identify each scene by number, so that you can easily find it.

This log should include not only the scenes where the script says that your character is present, but also the scenes where your character has no dialogue, but, by association with place, may appear in the shot. For instance, if you are the owner of a restaurant and many scenes take place in that restaurant, you may want to include these scenes in your log, because you may be a silent observer to the action of other characters' scenes. A silent observer is not a still, unthinking object in the background. An observer in a film is often an active participant or witness.

If there is a party scene and your character is in attendance, there may be times when you are in the background, and although the script hasn't given you anything to say or do, you should be prepared to have a relationship to your surroundings and to the people around you. You should also be clear about your relationship to the action portrayed in the scenes being performed by the characters that are given action and dialogue. These are just two examples of assuming your character's presence in a scene through association with place. There are many others and with little effort you will be able to identify them for yourself.

See your character as an inhabitant of the world in which the film takes place, a native, an active participant, not just an innocent bystander who every now and then steps into the spotlight when he or she has something to say.

OBSERVATIONS, THOUGHTS, AND JOURNAL NOTES

To create the world of the character, bring in aspects of your world that will help you. This could be any number of things, depending on what speaks to you the best. Notes from your research and observations should be included, as well as any other support material that inspires you. Include these things in the section that corresponds with the scene where this information might be helpful.

Keep a journal of your character preparations, and include in your log the quotes that reveal vital information to you. An insight that you have while working can appear complete and clear in your mind, and in that moment, you know exactly what you want to do with it in your acting. But on the set, with exhaustion and the pressures of filming, this same insight might get lost or thrown by the wayside. Keep track of these insights and be sure to include them in your log. You only need a small portion of a greater discovery to bring it back fully to the forefront of your mind. In the journal, you can write it all full out; in the log, a sentence or two or a picture will bring it back to full recall.

As I looked back on my various logs, I found many notes that surprised me. I used to make collages from magazine sheets that would describe something I was going after in the character that I could not yet express in words or in acting choices. These images would clarify various overriding facets in the character's life that inspired me. In some cases, when I had a more intimate relationship with the director, I would show her these collages as a sort of visual guide to bring about a further discussion of the character. Because the directors were more visually oriented than I was, they would often be able to understand the elements in my collages better than I did and offer some advice to realize these characters more fully. When I look at these collages now, they instantaneously bring back vital elements of the character I was working on at that time. The discoveries you make from playing one character will often do well for playing another, even though your application of them might be completely different.

Don't leave out whatever inspires you on your journey deeper into the existence of the person you will play. To know a concrete usage of an inspiration is not as important as being inspired; the usage will make itself evident at a later time.

TIME LINE: CONTINUITY

Each scene section should have a time line for your character. If the information is given to you in the script, by all means use it, but many times it is not specifically given; you have to make it up from the given circumstances of the screenplay. In doing so you are creating the life of the character when she is not seen in the script. You should note the following:

- The time of day.

- How much time has passed since we last saw the character?

- What do you think the character was doing when he or she was not on the screen?

- Where is the character coming from before the start of each scene? Pay particular attention to connecting scenes, like walking down the street or riding in buses or trains. These scenes may have no dialogue, but show the character in transit. Prepare something for each of these circumstances.

- Always answer the questions:

    Where am I coming from?

    Where am I now?

    Where am I going?

- Remember that film scenes are always occurring in the present moment. The audience is seeing what is unfolding at a particular moment in time, and that moment is now.

ENTRANCES

Entrances into rooms or locations can pose special problems. When you enter a scene in a film, you start from a stationary fixed point and begin moving when "action" is called. Sometimes, there is a count or a cue that you enter upon. There is no wing space on a set; you are usually cramped between light stands, sandbags, and cable coils. Where you are coming from and the condition of your character must be immediately seen upon your entry. In some cases this has to be practiced; you have no time to warm up into what you are going to do. You go from absolute stillness and inertia into the full moment.

Where you are coming from, as seen in the finished picture, might easily be a completely different location than where you are entering into, even though it will look like a continuous flow of time and place. This is where the character log comes in very handy. In order to make your character's life appear continuous, you need to be at first intellectually aware of your character's movement and then carry some form of preparation from the shooting of one scene into the shooting of the next. You do this regardless of how much time has passed between the shooting of the two scenes.

In the theater this continuity is achieved through decisions made in rehearsal. It is solidified and improved upon by the continuity of each performance. In film it is conceived, on one hand, by an elaborate engine of checks and balances of the film crew and postproduction team, and, on the other hand, by the actor's ability to create the illusion of a continuous life on the screen.

Some actors try and hold all of this information in their heads, and seem to have no trouble doing so. I find this difficult and prefer to write it all down where I can quickly check on the information and then clear my concentration for the focus of acting the scene. Successful actors may have assistants who, along with other duties, assist them in keeping everything straight, but most actors have to take care of it themselves. If you are playing a small part, it isn't difficult to remember a few bits of continuity information, but if your role is large, the amount of information can become enormous. It's best not to rely on the person who is doing continuity or the other members of the crew that you deal with; they have plenty of their own problems and will not have time to help you deal with yours.

PLACE

Once you have made a concerted effort to position your character in time, you can start to work on place. Go through each scene and see if you feel you need an imaginary parallel place for that scene. Many times you won't because the actions are so simple, but many times you may be called upon to exhibit very large and specific emotions and reactions to a place. In these instances some solid preparation may be a good idea. For instance, any scene that involves fear, apprehension, looking for something, or surprise, may require a place preparation. Any scene that is supposed to be taking place in a dark or shadowy location should definitely be prepared. Darkness doesn't exist in filmmaking; it only looks like that on the screen. Film, and even its modern cousin, digital video, require light. Where there is light there is a picture; where there is no light there is no picture; it's as simple as that. If the script says that you're walking down a dark, deserted alley at night, rest assured there will be enormous floodlights on you and the crew. You will have to reach into your own dark, deserted places and come up with one that you can project in the space around you. This is accomplished through the creation of a place sense memory. Sight and sound are the obvious choices here, but whichever of your senses brings back a place for you is the one you use. Each acting instrument is unique; each actor finds the way to interact best with his or her imaginary objects.

Another scenario where place should be used is if the actor is required to tell a story from memory and the script will edit back and forth between the flashback and the actor narrating the story. In this case the actor is a guide who leads the audience through the transition of seeing into her memory. It is a popular device in screenplays, and not such an easy one to accomplish from an acting point of view. We do this type of thing in life all the time and are often taken by surprise at the fullness of the emotional recall when recounting a memory. There are events in our past that we won't speak of because the recall is all too painful and too real. Recalling an experience of great happiness can produce unexpected responses of yearning for good times long gone. Observe what the nature of such an experience is in preparation for such a scene. The memory is easier to create if you have sensual recall happening in the moment that you are speaking.

You should thoroughly explore the intricacies of this emotional landscape in your preparation time before you attempt to use sense memory as a character element on a set. Journal work, for yourself and then for your character, is a good idea. Writing in a journal as the character while in the midst of a sense memory can be very useful in creating the character's inner life and history.

Go through the script and make sure you know where each scene takes place, and give some thought to the nature of each place and what behavior occurs there in everyday life. Make choices. Don't be a character drifting in space somewhere. Be as specific as possible; try and unlock the frozen assets of each location.

THE SENSUAL CHARACTER

Sensualize the world around the scene. Take note of all sensory elements that are mentioned in the script specifically and work on these elements either separately or within the context of the scene.

Check each scene for any mention of the five senses. We know what they are, but be hyperaware of them now. This would include elements of the environment, like heat and cold, as well as conditions of the body, like drunkenness or fatigue. If the scene takes place in a garden, take time to smell the roses. If your character has a hangover, be aware of what that condition does to you, and modify it for the character. In the previous chapters many of the senses were specifically discussed and exercises were given to enhance these senses in an acting context. Now you must take what is useful from those exercises and modify it for the context of the scene and the conditions of the character. Your log should contain any sense memory keys that you may want to incorporate into the scene.

CREATING RELATIONSHIP

When you rehearse a play, your relationship to the other characters is developed through the time and discoveries in the rehearsals. Films are rarely rehearsed; therefore each actor has to create relationship with the environment and the other characters through her imagination. Just because you don't have a scene with another character doesn't mean that you don't have a relationship to him. Relationships can be formed quickly on a film set, but you have to have given it some thought beforehand.

Ask yourself—what is the relationship? There are the obvious ones, the primal ones of mother and father, sister and brother, etc. There are the professional ones; teacher and student, boss and employee, policemen and civilian, etc. Extend your thinking of relationship beyond that. Question yourself about how you feel about the other people who inhabit the world created by the script and what is your place among them.

Some roles imply social position, but some don't; you have to surmise it. Every character is situated within a hierarchy of a social order. What

Creating the Character

your character's position is and how *you* feel about it affects all of your actions. There is no such thing as a character who has no relationships; there is always a choice involved. The more conscious you are of your character's choices, the easier it will be to realize her as a living human being.

The decisions you make about your relationship to the other characters should be included in the notes of your log. Remember that decisions are not written in stone and that posing a question that is not yet answerable is also a form of decision-making. Always permit yourself to be persuaded or convinced, just like you are in life.

NEEDS AND ACTIONS

Let's not forget all of the other acting axioms, such as finding the needs and actions of the character. When you find the action of the character, you have a motor that will drive the car through the scene. Film acting is still acting, even though it's done in disjointed little segments that finally make up the whole. Directors will often speak in terms of needs and actions of the character, or even of a scene. If you have identified what you would like to accomplish in your preparation time, you will have the ammunition to fulfill the requirements of your direction.

Many directors know quite a bit about acting technique, but they cannot be acting teachers on the set; it's too late for that. You, the actor, must be loaded with the ammunition of your talent and preparation. The director, like a general on the battlefield, simply tells you when and where to fire.

The actions and the needs of the character should be noted for each scene. Make the sentences short, to the point, and include an active verb. This way, on the set, you can look at your notes and quickly remember what you wanted to do.

The character log is a way of putting all the work together in one ordered place. You have a log of your character's journey that you can refer to on the set. You have a continuity of time and place, regardless of the order in which the scenes will be shot.

Be as creative and individual with your log as possible. Keep it simple and direct, so that the useful aspects of the log are clear and easy to find. It is your own personal blueprint for the building of your character, a professional tool of inspiration, and a compass in times of confusion and indecision.

REHEARSALS

The old adage that time is money takes on mammoth proportions in filmmaking. The time and money constraints present at every level make a rehearsal period for the cast of a film prior to production rare. There just isn't the time allotted to working with the actors in the way that it is done in the theater. Unless the script is of a classical nature, as in the filming of a Shakespearean play or some comparable text, little or no rehearsals take place.

Another reason, and perhaps the major one, is that the medium doesn't lend itself to rehearsal before all of the technical machinery is in place and the whole cast and crew are on the set. Then a rehearsal for the camera, the sound, and the lights, as well as for the actors, can feasibly take place. There is an element of immediacy when the camera rolls, when all of the creative juices come together at once. The actors are an integral part, around whom much of the activity circles, but they are only one part in many that have come together to make the film happen. It's only when everyone is there, standing together on the set, that the true film rehearsal takes place. This can be very unsettling to the inexperienced film actor who is accustomed to some kind of rehearsal process. The actor has to know how to work his instrument, his machinery, the same way the camera operator knows how to focus and work the camera, the same way each crew member knows her job. It is a world of technical proficiency and machinery. The fact that the actor's instrument is human only affords a slight amount of preferential treatment for failure, but not much.

There are forms of rehearsals that do take place, and I will try to cover them in this chapter. Of course each director has her own style of dealing with the problem of preparing the actors for their performances, but I will try to examine the most common experiences of the film actor. I will also give you some advice on what you can do on your own to fill the gaps when little or no rehearsal takes place.

THE READING

The most common way of rehearsing the actors is the reading. This is becoming more and more popular among directors as a means of communicating interpretations of the script and the individual characters to the actors. Directors develop their own style of conducting readings to get the most out of them. Some prefer a very relaxed setting, like an apartment or home, very often their own, where each scene is hashed out and talked about, perhaps the actors will improvise a little to further the discovery of the characters. Others go for a more formal setting of a rehearsal studio or office, where the screenplay is simply read and generally discussed for content.

Although there are many variations on the reading theme, most are conducted from a seated position, with no props or blocking. The concentration is on the text, the interpretation of the actor's approach to the text, and the relationships between the characters. Everything else will be taken care of when the actual day of shooting is at hand. Let's take a look at some possible reading scenarios and what you can do to get the most out of them.

INFORMAL ROUNDTABLE READING

I call this a roundtable because of its egalitarian feel. The whole idea is to meet one another in an atmosphere devoid of pressure. If you have been cast in a role and are asked to come to an informal reading of the script, you are very lucky. This means you will have an opportunity to meet your director and fellow cast members in a relaxed setting. Some directors invite various crew members to readings as well, especially the director of photography, costume designer, and assistant directors. If the director is not the author, the writer might be present to fix anything that needs fixing in the script.

There will be the usual introductions, probably some refreshments; always bring your own water in case none is provided. The director or someone else in charge will make a brief statement, and then you will open your script and the reading will start. The period of time before the reading begins is not the time to bring up a lot of questions for the director. It is a time of concentrated listening and observing. Unless you have a question of pronunciation, a truly technical confusion about the text, or a *very brief and simple* interpretation question, it's best to remain silent—just observe and listen. Many of your questions will be answered in the course of the reading itself.

The informal reading is a perfect opportunity to start to build the relationships that your character will have in the movie. Watch the other actors, and see how you fit into this world. Form opinions and make decisions. Allow yourself to be affected by the performance of any partners that you have. Whatever preparations you have made for the reading, grant the other characters permission to influence your moment-to-moment reality within your scenes. Give yourself over to the text. Don't be timid; if you have an idea, now is the time to try it out to its fullest extent. Always have a pencil with you at a reading to make quick notes in your script as you go along.

A few general rules of any reading:

- Allow the words to do the work for you.

- Don't illustrate, with any sort of actions, what is being read in the descriptive copy of the script.

- The only thing you have to do is read your lines and be emotionally present within the context of your scenes.

- You never act out anything that is being described about your character's behavior that is nonverbal or is being observed by other characters. Just sit still.

- Only come to life as your character when you have text or are part of a scene.

- However, if you do have a role with a lot of nonverbal activity, you might want to ask the director what to do when that copy is being read. She may want you to indicate something of the action.

When the reading is over, the general discussion usually begins. It is here that the questions can be asked about interpretation. If the director is beaming and looks at you and says, "That's great, you were wonderful, thank you so much, I have nothing to say," she probably means it, and whatever you did is in accord with the director's vision. What this actually means is you should keep working in the same direction to further develop the character. It does not mean that you stop working and assume there's nothing more to do until you're called to the set.

When the director does give you a note, then you are expected to fix it on your own by the time you get to the set. If you don't know how to do it, then you will have to hire a coach who specializes in film, one who will know how to help you find the technical solution to your problem. There will be no time to fix it once shooting starts.

Never take a note or direction from another actor or, for that matter, from anyone other than the director. By the same token, never give another actor a note or direction—always stay within the circle of your own instinct under the guidance of the director. I would be very wary of any actor who starts suggesting line changes or interpretation tips for *your* character, regardless of who he is. Actors should only take care of their own parts.

The informal reading is also a perfect opportunity to become aware of any text difficulties that need to be addressed. Whatever pitfalls there may be for you, they will have to be corrected before your shooting begins. Some films offer a dialogue coach to help cast members with accents or special concerns of the text. This only happens on the bigger-budget films and is, of course, wonderful for the actor.

When the reading is over, you should set aside some time to write in your journal and make further notes in your script. Do this fairly soon after the reading—your ideas should be fresh in your mind.

GOING THROUGH THE SCRIPT SCENE BY SCENE

In a very good scenario, the director may want to separately work on scenes that demand more attention. Often these scenes are of a complex emotional nature or have unique timing, and the director would like to put the actors through their paces as one might in a theatrical situation. This is wonderful when it happens; all the acting problems can be ironed out in advance. Improvisational techniques may come into play here, depending on the training of the director and how much she knows about actors. Improvisation can highlight aspects of the character that will have to be acutely demonstrated later, on the set, in a much more economic fashion. It can also free up the inner life of the characters by widening the range of possibilities that might have been hidden before. More in-depth discussions may take place at these smaller meetings, and many questions you might have had can be talked about and answered.

During such a rehearsal, you may be able to employ the Inner Monologue to express what you would like to communicate with the text, but are unable to convey. You can only use this technique sparingly, and then revert immediately back to the text to try and put into the text what you have just said in your own words. It is a way of uncovering a moment when there is no time to discuss or hash it out. The impulse comes through your own words and then goes right into the line that you are supposed to say. Sometimes talking too much about these moments can dissipate the momentum of the impulse. It's best to stay within the concentration of the scene, while you allow a glimmer of your inner intent to shine into the text, through your own words.

Al Pacino made a film called *Looking for Richard* that illustrates this technique of wondering and exploring the questions you have about a character in a reading rehearsal. The movie, which is about Al's quest to understand how to present the Shakespearean play *Richard III* to an American audience, as well as his own grappling with playing the lead part himself, has wonderful scenes of his and his colleagues' approach to discovering a role. Many of the scenes that we see being rehearsed and discussed are then shown in their filmed performance. It took Al a year or so to make this film, which he did in bits and pieces, with different casts, in between his major motion picture roles. *Looking for Richard* shows a rare luxury of time that the vast majority of films in pre-production cannot afford. It also shows the power of the actors' inquisitive natures and their search to discover the inner lives of their characters while trying to decipher a text. I would highly recommend watching it.

Unfortunately, smaller scene rehearsals may not occur until the movie is already in its shooting phase, because of the demanding time constraints placed on a director in pre-production. They might occur a few days or even the night before you are scheduled to shoot the scene—they are dropped in as time allows, while the crew is setting up another shot or the weather has forced the cancellation of an exterior shoot. If this is the case, the rehearsal will be very economical. It will be a situation where, basically, the director tells you what she wants, and you have an opportunity to sit with your scene partners—as I've mentioned before it could be the first time you've actually met them. You go back to the rules of the informal reading—you mostly listen and observe—absorbing as much vital information as is possible that will be useful for playing the character. Always follow the lead of the director's style of distributing information and decipher how best to use it for your own means.

In the case of a film like *Apocalypse Now*, where the script is being worked on as you are making the movie and the lines of the relationship between actors, the characters that they are playing, the director, and the script become blurred in a net of discovery, both personal and professional, there are no rules. The rules are made up as you go along. The documentary by Eleanor Coppola about the making of *Apocalypse Now*, which she called *Hearts of Darkness: A Filmmaker's Apocalypse*, is an extreme example of what can happen when a director decides to go down this particular creative path. Francis Ford Coppola had already made *The Godfather* and *The Godfather II,* as well as many other films, before he started work on *Apocalypse Now*. He had also won several Academy Awards and written many screenplays for hire. Even with this breadth of experience, the problems he encountered during the making of this film are of legendary proportions.

The documentary shows the entire process he undertook and its affect on the actors, the screenplay, his family, and himself. From an acting point of view, it is very intriguing to watch how the actors fit into this process and what a large role they played in the development of the final film. To work with a director so uniquely committed to his vision that he will take everyone involved down such a creatively invigorating path, *and* who has such respect for the art of acting, can be every actor's dream. If the director lacks the experience and wisdom to pull off such an undertaking, it can be an actor's nightmare. It takes the willingness to experience a little of both dream and nightmare to survive being part of such enterprise, regardless of its outcome.

THE STAGED SCREENPLAY READING

The staged screenplay reading is a strange animal within the film world. It is becoming increasingly popular as an entertainment form of its own and is actually closer kin to a public performance of a radio play than to the viewing of a film. You *hear* the film, see the actors who are speaking the parts, but really, it is the audience's imagination that brings the film to life; they *see* the pictures in their minds. This is why it is more like a radio play than a film. The reason I include it under the chapter for rehearsals is, it might be the only rehearsal you get before you start shooting, when you will have camera rehearsals on the set.

The actors sit across the stage in a line. Each wears a head microphone, and a narrator at one end reads all of the slug lines and copy descriptions. There is usually no movement of the actors and no props. It is through the descriptive copy and the voices of the characters that the story is conveyed. Theater actors and voice-over artists are often employed to do the staged reading, because the voice is so important to getting the story across.

These readings only have one read-through rehearsal, usually done on the same day as the actual performance. Normally, you have gotten your script a week in advance, and, though you are not expected to memorize anything, you are expected to act as you read. At the rehearsal you should pace yourself, for you'll have to perform it again at the public reading. I know that in the theater actors do matinee and evening performances, but that is a different process altogether. In the theater, the play has been rehearsed; therefore you know what you have to do and you have learned through rehearsals how to gauge your performance. In the case of the staged reading rehearsal, you can, at first, only learn what will be expected of you by putting your main energy into listening and observing where the difficulties will lie for the actual performance. Then you quickly make the necessary decisions and choices in the comparatively short break between the rehearsal and the performance. Once you're on stage, you simply go with what you've got and leave any worrying about how to fix it if it's wrong, out of your sphere of concentration for the moment.

The director will seat each cast member in the right position for his character. Usually you will stay in the same chair throughout the reading. There might be times when your scene partner or partners will be down at the other end of the seating line, and although you can glance at them or address them, you'll have to primarily keep your face and body open to the audience. The trouble always is gauging just the right amount of energy to convey your emotions from a seated position while facing out front, rather than facing your scene partner.

The actors don't move, because it takes away from the imaginary world the audience members are creating in their minds. It disturbs their concentration. If there is a great deal of movement, the audience will expect more than can be delivered from actors sitting and holding their scripts. It's much better to keep things fairly still and allow the magic of the script to work through the images of the words. Besides, if you're wired to a head mike, every change in seating would require you to take off your mike, move to another seat, and put on a new mike. This would definitely break up the flow of the screenplay. Screenplay readings are miked, not only because it adds to the illusion of watching a film by electronically amplifying the voice, but also because they often take place in spaces like movie theaters or small auditoriums that are acoustically unfit for theatrical voice projection.

Regardless of your distance from your partner, you must place your concentration on the moment-to-moment reality of the scene. Since it is miked, you can use your voice appropriately for the scene's requirements. The descriptive copy might state that the two of you have just woken up from a passionate night and your scene is a sweet repartee of two people discovering one another. Even though you are sitting at one end and your partner at the other, you'll have to convey the intimacy of two lovers in bed. This is good practice for the close-up shot, where you will have to act, without seeing your partner, to the camera. On the other hand, if you are supposed to be in a barroom brawl, you will not be able to physically demonstrate through actions. You'll have to convey the majority of the reality through your voice, with only minimal movement. The narrator will be describing the physical action by reading the descriptive copy. An animated, engaged, and well-paced narrator is an essential component to a staged reading's success.

In Shakespeare's day I've heard it was said, "I'm going to *hear* a play," rather than, "I'm going to *see* a play." Thus the emphasis was on the words and what they might evoke. This is also true of the staged reading, though it has another aspect in common with Shakespeare's time— the custom of doubling. A straight line across a small stage can only hold about fifteen chairs, and even that's quite crowded. Some scripts have many characters with just a few lines, like the roles of Policeman #1 and #2, Waitress, or Lady with a Dog, etc. They can't have twenty different actors playing each role at the reading, as they will have in the finished film, so actors double, triple, quadruple, etc., roles. Every character in a screenplay reading needs a voice and someone has to be assigned that role. Sometimes that's all you'll do in a reading, read all the little parts appropriate to your gender. I think I once played about fifteen one- or two-liner roles in a staged reading about a detective gone bad in New York City. I made up a different character for each of the roles. I had an absolute blast doing every accent and voice type I could think of. I was very lucky that the setting was New York City, though, because every-body in the world lives and works in New York City. If you find yourself in a reading with a ton of little characters to play, enjoy yourself, and give each character their moment in the sun.

The staged reading is also used as a marketing tool to generate funds and attention for a project that is trying to lure investors and producers. Very often stars or their representatives will attend a reading to see if they are interested in the material. It is a very economical approach to generating interest in a film looking to be made. What this means to actors is that being in a reading does not necessarily secure you a role in the film. You might play a lead in the reading and be asked down the road to play a much smaller role in the film, if you are involved in it at all. Don't be hurt or feel there's something wrong with your acting; accept that these things happen in the business all the time, and take the job. The road to getting a film made is a very rocky one, and there are many factors, mostly financial, that figure into the casting of lead characters. However, readings are always another form of auditioning. Just as they are a way of generating interest in a film, they can also generate interest in an actor.

I think the screenplay reading is becoming so popular because it constricts the actor the same way that a close-up does. In a reading, there's just enough distance between the actor and the audience to allow each audience member to enhance the performance with her own imag-ination. It brings the audience into the process. They are engaged—they become director, set designer, and director of photography as they create the film in their minds—they feel that their input is needed to complete the creation of the film. Indeed, they are needed at this moment. As the actor, you have a chance to feel out the character as it will feel when you stand alone before the void of the camera lens. In this strange way the staged reading is like a public rehearsal; it is a way of testing your public privacy when you are engaged within the concentration of your character's world.

A relaxed, breathing, open actor sitting there before an audience is a very compelling thing. Still but present, the actor leads the audience into his character with the ambience of his voice and the subtlety of his movement. It is a very seductive relationship. As with any seduction, if you over-do it, you will cross over the boundaries and lose your allure.

The minimalist approach is best as far as preparation goes for a staged reading. Here are a few pointers:

- Know the story and understand the screenplay as best as you can.

- Break down each of your scenes carefully and know exactly where the climaxes are.

- Think of your character as a piece of music. Vary the voice quality; don't play just one note.

- Highlight all of your text!

- Do voice warm-ups before the rehearsal and the performance. There usually isn't an intermission, so it might be two or more hours straight on stage.

- Get a good night's sleep the day before.

- Keep all sensory elements to a minimum, unless you are very proficient at them. You can't get distracted or involved with your own thing; you've got to stay with the pack.

- Let the words come out of the impulse, and stay in the moment with your partner.

- Choose a few simple traits that are within the character, and accentuate them. Don't try and create the entire movie. It's impossible from a chair, with a script in your hand, while you're wearing a head mike.

- Work fully within the limitations.

• Stay in the moment, and go with the flow.

• Have a very good time.

SCRIPT DEVELOPMENT THROUGH REHEARSAL AND IMPROVISATION

Some projects have a long gestation period, either through the creative methods of the director/writer or because of necessity; it just takes a long time to work out what the script is really about. Actors may be called in to help with the development of a screenplay. Both films I mentioned before, *Looking for Richard* and *Hearts of Darkness*, present good examples of how actors and directors work together to complete the script development process. If you have never worked on a film script in this way, I would jump at any opportunity that might come your way, even if you never get to be in the finished film. Of course you'd have to like and respect the people that you're working with. Many student directors or groups of friends will get together to try and collaboratively work on a script. If you become involved with such a process, the sensory work of the earlier chapters can be of a real value.

The director/writer supplies an intellectual format or concept that may or may not have yet taken the form of a script. The actors take the concept on a journey through their imaginary reality as the concept inspires them. Their imaginary reality elucidates different factors of the creative concept through action and behavior. This bounces back to the writer/director, who formalizes it and throws it back into the acting pit by either structuring it into a script or making the concept more complex. The video camera is often brought into these rehearsals to record and experiment with the visual style. This process can go back and forth over a long period of time. Because you work together so intensely, very enduring relationships, both professional and private, can come from sharing this process. It can be a wonderfully rewarding experience that should be enjoyed solely for its own sake.

It takes a very special creative personality to formulate all of the process work into a script that can be the blueprint for a viable movie. Many films that look as though they have been improvised have come into being through this process; at some point, the director/writer pulls it all together into a cohesive whole. What you are seeing on the screen, which appears so spontaneous, is actually the result of years of planning and work.

However, many groups that embark upon exploratory projects find that there is no end to the exploration—it just goes on and on—they fall in love with the process, and the film never gets finished. In spite of this being the case, I would still strongly suggest becoming involved in such a project at least once, if the opportunity arises and you can afford the time (one is rarely paid for such labors of love). It is invaluable as a learning tool, and it gives you an opportunity to see inside the creative structure of the director/writer/actor relationship and how it works within the film medium. The knowledge you can gain from this experience will be extremely useful for the rest of your film career.

THINGS TO DO ON YOUR OWN

If you can't rehearse with the director or other cast members, you can still improvise on your own. Without the overseeing eye of the director, though, the work can only be considered improvisational, because whatever you do might be changed once the filming starts.

Most actors do not exist in a vacuum; they are part of a community of other actors. The first thing you need is a trusted a friend or colleague who knows your work and will be willing to assist you. The person must agree to be there for you, that is, to help you prepare. You can't allow yourself to be directed in this process; you just need an assistant to play the other parts and bounce around your preparations, so you can find things on your own.

Here are a few approaches and tips to rehearsing on your own:

- Single out one or two things per rehearsal that you would like to work on. *No more than two!* To start with, you might chose exploring the nature of the relationship between you and a scene partner.

- Pose questions that you will try to answer through your improvisational work with your partner. Always go into an improvisation with a question that will set up a parameter within which to explore.

To improvise without parameters can be a waste of time. As in the sense memory work, it is best to *wonder* about the possibilities by giving your imagination free reign within a set of boundaries. You set up the boundaries by asking a specific question, rather than trying to prove a preconceived idea by forcing it on the improvisation. The right question will lead you to a usable answer or to the formulation of a better question. You only work on one or two elements at a time, so that you can explore them fully without overtaxing the acting instrument. You keep what you feel has worked from one improvisation, choose something else to work on, and layer it into the next improvisation.

Rehearsals

- Read the scene together, inserting the Inner Monologue when you don't understand something, either of your own text or of your partner's. Your partner should do this also.

- Use the Inner Monologue when you can't express with the text what you are actually feeling. Never bottle up your emotions or try to funnel them into a narrow, constricted idea of the character in a session with a friend. Listen to your impulses and express them.

Part of the reason that you bother to rehearse on your own is to give yourself more freedom than you will have in the professional situation. It gives you a chance to warm up to the character and work out the bugs. If you sanction a more permissive range of expression now, you will be able to uncover the problems with your preparation before you get to the set. Once uncovered, a problem can usually be solved.

- Try to find a situation that you are familiar with that is *like* the one in the screenplay and discuss it with your partner.

- Use this situation along with the one or two things you have isolated to explore the scene.

- Take your time. Don't worry about pacing and the rhythm of the scene.

If you have been developing the character, you might want to try some of your ideas out with your friend's help. See if you can create any of the sense memories you have chosen while looking into another pair of human eyes. You may find that your preparation will have to be adjusted when it encounters the opposition of another living being. It's one thing to be brilliant alone in your bedroom, quite another to hold your own against the forces of a scene partner. You want to check for tension here. Make sure that your preparation is not so strong that the emotion chokes you or so timid that it dissipates when you start putting some of the demands of the scene on it. You also want to make sure that you can remain flexible enough to respond to the other actor.

- Improvise the scenes that do not take place in the script but are part of the character's known history. This can either be events that take place before the character's life as it appears in the script or events that we know have occurred but are not shown in the movie.

This can be very valuable work to create a believable character. It also clarifies relationships that you have in the movie by making a history. When you do this type of improvisation, keep it simple and always have a good time; have fun.

The trick is to find out what you can use practically and eliminate that which bogs the character down in any form of self-indulgence or takes you away from the action of the scene. In order to do this you need to isolate the elements and work on them separately before you can layer the part into a cohesive whole.

Don't allow your partner to direct you or give you advice on how to play the part. Remember that the only opinion that really counts is that of your director, and you will have to wait to receive that one. The work you do on your own can strengthen your confidence and give you a battalion of ideas that you can pull from as needed on the set. It makes you feel less vulnerable and more prepared to perform once the camera starts rolling.

I love the art of the screenplay and how this wonderfully compact, precise written form opens the door to creative choices through its clear-cut, crisp format. I have tried, in these last chapters, to help the actor to get the most out of the script before the shooting starts and to help him to use his technique to create the character from the information in the script.

In the next segment of the book, I'll talk about the shooting of the movie, the roles that important crew members play for the actor, and how the actor works in the whirlwind that is a movie set.

PART THREE

THE SHOOT

BIG-BUDGET VERSUS LOW-BUDGET FILMS

As an actor, my point of view of filmmaking has always been from in front of the camera and all that it entails to become camera-ready. When I first started working in movies all I knew about filmmaking was what I had learned from the experience of being a spectator. Everything I thought came from my own personal experience of watching movies; my own taste and the performances of actors that I liked formed my opinion. If the movie did not entertain me, didn't evoke some kind of emotion or philosophical response in me, then I didn't like it. If I enjoyed it or it moved me in some way, then I liked it. I never considered the style, the photography, or the editing as being important. I wasn't really aware of the essential roles they played in my enjoyment of the movie. I wasn't aware of how movies were made. All I knew was that I loved watching movies, and I wanted to be in them.

When I started working in front of the camera, there was one other thing that I knew that was essential—how to act within my own circle of concentration and how to use my imagination in my acting. I soon started to learn more about the jobs of the others around me on the set. We were all part of one desire: to make the movie the best that we knew how, with each person concentrating on their own job. My job was that of the actor.

In the beginning, I played very small parts in big movies and lead parts in student and no/low-budget films. I wasn't yet a member of the Screen Actors Guild, and I was working in Europe, so there were no restrictions on what parts I could take. I worked on experimental video projects with no scripts and did scenes for film production classes in schools. I took any opportunity I got to be in front of the camera and be on a set. As long as I trusted the people I was working with not to exploit me in any harmful way, I was willing to put myself into whatever situation was necessary to learn more about acting in film and get in front of the camera. As my experience grew, I naturally became more discerning in my role choices, but at the start I was pretty much willing to go anywhere and do whatever was asked of me.

Because I had a lot of friends who were at the Film and Television Academy in Berlin I would often have the opportunity to be actively involved with the script development process. I was included in discussions when the other crew members would discuss how the script could be photographed, how the set would be designed, and which locations to use. Many times I was allowed to see the rushes (sometimes called dailies, because they are the unedited raw footage of the day's shooting) with the crew. If I knew the director very well, I would visit him while he was editing and converse with him about his editing choices.

The apartment where I lived was very spacious. Some of my roommates were filmmakers, and many of the first films I did were shot in this apartment. I found that the more I learned about movies, the more I wanted to know. I learned to respect everyone's input, and slowly, as I worked on bigger and more expensive projects with strangers, I learned where my job as an actor fell in the hierarchy of moviemaking. I loved every aspect of the collaborative art of moviemaking—I loved being photographed, I loved acting in front of the camera. I began to enjoy every kind of moving image presented on a screen, whether it was telling a story or merely existing for its own artistic sake, as my appreciation for the craft of filmmaking widened.

UNDERSTANDING FILMMAKING

Knowing or understanding how movies are made and what to expect while making them will not necessarily make you a better actor, but, if nothing else, it helps you to communicate with your director and comprehend what is happening around you. You become part of the milieu, you speak the language, you stay out of the way, and you know how to behave on the set. Understanding how movies are made helps you focus your attention on your job as the actor. It helps you to do a better job.

I am not a filmmaker, so there are many things about the making of films that I do not understand. People who are filmmakers, whether they are seasoned professionals or novices learning their craft, try to keep abreast of all of the exciting technological advances—in fact, it becomes a life-long pursuit. As an actor, you are concerned more with the execution and development of your own acting, rather than how it will be photographed. However, there is much information that is useful and will help you to be better equipped for the experiences and procedures that you encounter as you begin to work in front of the camera. I will try to break down some of the experiences in different types of filmmaking, from the student film to the Hollywood movie, to help you prepare more efficiently and to fit into the environment around you.

USING THE WORD "FILM"

I would like to clarify why I use the word "film" even though many of the important movies of today are being shot on digital video and other mediums. There is a lot of discussion in the entertainment industry today about the advance of digital technology and how it will affect filmmaking, both now and in the future. Cameras are becoming smaller and more versatile, and there are affordable computer programs to edit whatever you have shot; for relatively less money than ever before, almost anyone can call himself or herself a filmmaker. There are those who are saying that film is dead and everything will be digital video in the near future. No one knows what the future will bring for certain. We know it will bring change, but in what direction and how it will change is always an unknown.

It's interesting to note that in 1956 the entertainment publication *Daily Variety* had as a page one headline, "Film Is Dead!" above an article announcing the invention of videotape. Certainly, videotape changed many things in the entertainment industry; it broadened the possibilities. It did not, however, kill film. Today many have the opinion that anyone can make a movie, now that you don't need expensive lights, film stock, a large crew, and a studio. Just pick up the camera and shoot. The question remains the same regardless of what medium you use—shoot what? What is the story you are telling? How is that story best represented in images? An easy-to-use camera does not answer these questions by itself. The creative artist behind the camera still must answer them. It's true that the widespread availability of more inexpensive, lighter, and easier-to-use equipment broadens the spectrum of opportunity to those that it might have eluded before, but technology is only a tool for talent; it does not do the job for you.

The technology has made certain things easier, but it will not give you great ideas. Having a pen does not make you a great writer, nor does knowing how to type or to use a computer. Shakespeare wrote with a quill, and he managed to be rather prolific with very crude tools by today's standards.

Each generation finds new ways of telling their stories. Each generation wants to separate itself from the past, and that is quite understandable. But even in the modern world of filmmaking, the actor is still standing in front of a camera, and light in some form is still necessary for an image, unless the entire movie is shot in night vision. Styles may change, but the content, what the story is trying to say, and how that story is composed in images is still very important.

The general consensus is that whatever the format, whether it be photochemical film, digital video, or computer-generated images, the

Big-Budget versus Low-Budget Films

process is still called filmmaking. We still say, *I shot my film* on digital video. So for purposes of clarity and brevity, unless I'm making a technical point about a specific medium, I will refer to all projects as "movies" or "films," regardless of the stock or format that was used to produce the images in them. Indeed, many films today use a variety of mediums to create the look that is right for the movie. The actor is not consulted on these decisions and, as always, she has to follow the instructions of the director.

ALL FILMS ARE THE SAME

Regardless of the budget, all film sets have the same problems; big-budget films just solve them more expensively. The same kinds of questions have to be answered by the filmmakers. There are millions of decisions that have to be made at each step along the way. With a bigger budget, acclaimed craftspeople, and an experienced crew, problems might be solved with more money, expertise, or artistry, but the basic dilemmas are still the same. The same questions arise no matter the budget or the film medium.

- What is the film about?

- How will it be told in pictures?

- Where is the camera going to be placed?

- What are the angles and camera movements that best tell this story?

- What and where is the light source?

The film set, whether it is in a studio with 70mm film or on a street corner with a handheld digital video camera, poses the same problems for the actor. Where is the camera, where is the light, and what am I supposed to be doing while the film is rolling? If you begin thinking of it in these practical terms, it's much easier to take the pressure off and adjust, whatever the circumstances. If you think of it as Jodie Foster does, as a blue-collar job, you can easily place your concentration on the practical problems of the moment, rather than on the imaginary successes and failures of the future.

There are three phases that a film goes through once the decision has been made to shoot a script. Some form of each of these stages must take place to create the finished film. The actor is mostly involved in the shooting phase of the film, when photography takes place, but may be called in as needed at other times.

PREPRODUCTION

The planning stage of the movie. The locations are scouted, the crew is hired, and the major part of casting is done. A production office is set up that becomes the headquarters for the film. All special equipment is ordered; problems and travel plans are discussed. The shooting schedule for the movie is planned, and the different departments meet to find out what the demands on them will be. The more meticulously a film is planned, the better everything else will go once shooting starts. Aside from the casting process, an actor may be called in for hair, makeup, and costume tests during this period. If you are very lucky, rehearsals might even take place during this time.

PRODUCTION

The period of time in which the photography of the film actually takes place. The average feature-length film takes about six to eight weeks to shoot. The production office is still the main headquarters through which all information flows. Obviously, this is the phase that involves the actor.

POSTPRODUCTION

Sometimes referred to as "post." This is the assembly of the material that has been photographed into what eventually becomes the finished film that we see. This includes the editing, the sound mix, special effects, and sometimes the shooting of additional scenes that the director now feels are needed to complete the film. The actor may be called in for these scenes or for looping, which is filling in dialogue in a studio synced to your own screen image.

There is, of course, another phase: the distribution and marketing of the film, which eventually brings it to the viewer. This phase is not covered in this book, although the actor may be called in to promote the film for publicity purposes.

STUDENT FILMS

Let's take a look at the different types of film projects, starting at the beginning with the student film. Everyone has to start somewhere, and film school is where many filmmakers start. It's not a bad place to begin acting in front of a camera, either. You can think of student films as a sort of scene class for screen acting. Many people teach film acting with a single video camera on a tripod, but there is a limited amount that you can learn from that. In fact, some of what you learn from such an experience will not translate onto a set and into the film medium. I think that student film projects are a great place to work for a variety of actors.

- It's a good place to start if you are a novice actor or have never acted in films.

- It's a good place for actors who have been away from the business for a long time and want to start working again.

- I think it can also be a good place to hone those elements of your technique that you have not been satisfied with in your previous film work.

A student film is made by someone in film school who is making the film as part of the school's curriculum. There are many different levels of these projects and it's always a good idea to know what level and type of project it is before you get involved. There is almost never payment; it's usually meals, transportation, and a copy of the tape. The meals will be bagels or peanut butter and jelly, the transportation usually an overcrowded second-hand car, and the tape (a copy of the film on VHS) may prove to be much more difficult to actually get into your hands than you ever could have imagined. That being said, these projects can be a lot of fun, very creative, and you might be lucky enough to create a lifelong friendship that will translate professionally later in your career. You are usually truly appreciated for being a participant, even if your director has no idea what to say to you as an actor. After all, you are really part of his dreams coming true.

Following are some different types of student projects you might encounter. Most film schools are four-year programs for undergraduate or two- or three-year programs on the Master's level. Obviously, the later the year, the more proficient the student.

THE PRODUCTION CLASS PROJECT

Film schools have production classes, where the students learn all the jobs of the film crew as they shoot small projects. Usually, these are assignments with an instructor present during class time. In the second or third year, the production class starts to bring in actors from the outside; before that, the students shoot each other. It's usually a simple exercise, like coming into a room, or a small scenario, lasting a minute or two of screen time. The shooting of such a project takes about six hours.

The actor is usually responsible for her own clothing and makeup, all of which has been discussed and agreed upon beforehand. There isn't a great deal of pressure to perform, because the emphasis of the production class is on the techniques of filmmaking, not on the performance and direction of the actor. It's a good place to start if you have never been in front of the camera, because you can become accustomed to being on the set and start to decipher the crew positions. The atmosphere is generally very relaxed, because everyone is just learning what to do. You can also learn a great deal from the instructor if he lectures during the process. Call the school directly to inquire about how it finds actors for production classes.

THE FIRST-, SECOND-, OR THIRD-YEAR FILM PROJECT

These are small films that each student is required to make in order to proceed to the next level. As you might guess, they can vary widely, depending on the talent and maturity of the student. These projects could take place anywhere and are shot by the student director and his classmates. They are usually about ten to twenty minutes in length. They could be crude or elaborate, depending on the creativity and the finances of the director. Sometimes the scripts can be lovely, dealing with daring subjects and issues. However, because these are student projects, the script may not be realized as clearly as you might desire. The time involved often exceeds expectations (this happens on all films), so you have to be prepared for that. Obviously, the later the year, the more experienced the student. As an actor, you can use the projects to:

- See how your technique responds under the duress of the set and the seemingly tedious repetition of multiple takes.

- Understand why relaxation and concentration is so important.

- Begin to learn about the importance of lighting and how you work with it.

- Try out your ideas about creating a character for the screen.

- Take chances in your acting that you might be afraid to risk in a more professional and high-profile setting.

- Ask to view the raw footage (the rushes) of your various takes, so that you can learn from them. You must promise to be quiet and not interfere with decisions of the director if you are permitted to do this.

THE THESIS FILM

The thesis film is the final project of the undergraduate film student before graduation. This is the project that every student filmmaker hopes will be his or her passport into the profession. This film is meant for the public, and film schools exhibit them in a theater around the time of graduation.

A thesis production can be very close to making a real movie, and if you have a lead role, it could be a sizeable time commitment. I would suggest asking the director if you could see some of his previous work, and then make the decision if you want to be involved or not. His work doesn't have to be perfect, or commercial, but it should exhibit some ability to tell a story and have a point of view. These are often cast through the traditional avenues of casting directors and the trades, or from the pool of people that the director knows and has worked with before.

THE GRADUATE THESIS FILM

A graduate student's thesis project is the crown jewel of student films. These films are usually quite developed, since the students are more mature and have studied a great deal. They are usually clearer about what they would like to say in film. The professors at the graduate level are often famous filmmakers who mentor the students through their films.

Martin Scorsese attended New York University's first graduate film class. His thesis project was a sixty-five-minute piece called *Bring on the Dancing Girls* and starred Harvey Keitel. It wasn't well-received, but it showed he had promise. Two years after he graduated, an instructor of Scorsese's from NYU put his own money into the film and convinced him to go back and rework it. After six months of rewrites and the addition of new scenes, the film was renamed *Who's That Knocking at My Door,* with Harvey Keitel again starring. It took five years for this process to complete itself. Scorsese made a sequel to it several years later called *Mean Streets,* starring Harvey Keitel and Robert de Niro.

There is no way of telling if the student director that you begin to work with will turn out to be a director of the caliber of Martin Scorsese or if your relationship with him will be as satisfying and lasting as the ones he developed with Keitel and especially with DeNiro, but one always dreams. I would suggest watching *Mean Streets* to see the work of a young, talented director at work telling a story that he knows well with actors whom he loves. It will help you to train your eye to gauge the work of other beginning directors.

NO/LOW-BUDGET FILMS

A no- or low-budget film is basically a project that doesn't really have enough money to get made, but everyone crosses their fingers, uses imagination, begs, borrows, yes even steals, and prays that the thing makes it to the finish line. Such a film could be a short (these are enjoying a comeback due to cable and the Internet), or of feature length. There are many stories about these projects that go on to bring fame and fortune to all involved. There are many more stories of movies started that are never finished, or worse, finished and never seen. When you work on a no/low-budget film, you have to do it for the love of the moment, and not because you think it will make you a star. You should do it because you love to work; besides, you always gain experience and some exposure.

Conditions on no/low-budget movies can vary widely, depending on the experience and care of the director and his or her crew and production staff. Regardless of how much care is taken, the work will almost certainly be grueling. Eventually, exhaustion will set in. It's in this state that the actor has to remember to specifically go back to the relaxation and concentration, perhaps now more than ever. There could be chaos around you, but you will have to stay within the scope of your own job, acting, and remain focused and calm.

SHOOTING RATIO

The shooting ratio is taken from the total amount of film or footage that is shot. It is the ratio between the footage that is actually used in the film to the footage that was shot but not used. It is not unlikely for a major feature to have the luxury of shooting at a 15:1 ratio. That means they shoot fifteen times more film than they will actually use in the edited movie. In a no/low-budget film, you're lucky to be working with a shooting ratio somewhere between 5:1 and 2.5:1. That strains everybody's nerves, because there is very little room for mistakes. The director does a lot of nail biting, because if he doesn't pay attention to the amount of film that gets used each day, he won't have enough money to finish the film. If he doesn't pay enough attention to the scenes that are being shot, he will have material that isn't good enough to be used, and he won't be able to reshoot. The production company just doesn't have the money.

As an actor, you can't do anything about this, except be aware that every time you step in front of the camera when the film is rolling, you have to give it your all. You should also be aware of the enormous strain that is on the director, caused by lack of funds, and seek to understand the best way you can work to accomplish your job.

HOW A LOW BUDGET AFFECTS THE ACTOR

There are many things that directly affect you on a low-budget shoot:

- The look of the character is often left largely to the actor to create. You may be asked to use your own clothing, which you

Big-Budget versus Low-Budget Films

certainly don't have to do if you don't want to. Many actors really enjoy using their own belongings for a character, because they feel that they are truly creating from their own raw materials and making a statement. They become excited about creating the look of their character. It can be very exhilarating, but it can also be very time-consuming and expensive.

One thing I would suggest: Never use anything of your personal belongings on a film shoot that you aren't prepared to either lose or have destroyed. It doesn't matter if the director and crew have promised you that all of your things will be taken good care of, it's a promise that can't be kept on the lower end of filmmaking. On a big-budget film, you wouldn't be asked to use anything of your own.

- Personal problems have a tendency to arise on the set—since there isn't a lot of money for the casting process, directors will often use people whom they know, friends and family members. Many of the locations and props might stem from these relationships. These personal relationships between cast, crew, and the location can make for an interesting mix of events. The line between your life, the character that you are playing, and your exhausted imagination can blur while shooting.

- There could be very poor facilities to do essential things. A low-budget shoot does not have trailers. Trailers are what supply all of the amenities, like bathrooms, makeup mirrors and tables with proper lights, places to change clothing, places to sleep or rest. If you don't have a trailer, you're using the sleazy bar on the corner's bathroom and changing your clothes in the back of a van while the crew checks out their equipment. Modesty can be a real problem factor in these cases.

- The director and crew can completely forget about the actor. I know this sounds bizarre, but I have been in situations where the crew was finished with a scene, and no one told me that I was no longer needed for the shooting of that scene. The crew is much smaller on a low-budget, so it's often missing the important liaison crew member who communicates what's happening on the set to the actors. This can be particularly troublesome if you are on a location somewhere, in costume, and there is no one to take care of you while you wait or watch over your personal effects while you are shooting. If you are worried about your personal safety, it's hard to concentrate fully on acting. When you act, you are vulnerable in a very special way; your defenses are down in a way that you don't normally allow when you go about your daily life. If you feel that this aspect of your job reality is not taken seriously or acknowledged, then you have to bring it up to either a production assistant or to the director. Usually, it's just on oversight. They figure you're a grown up, you can take care of yourself, and lack of experience makes them think that they have more important things to worry about.

I was once shooting a scene for a very low-budget video project with a friend of mine as the director. We were shooting in our apartment, and the cameraman was her ex-boyfriend. We had been shooting for over eight hours, and it was about two in the morning when they suddenly had a very bad disagreement about whether or not they needed more shots from a different angle. She wanted it, he thought it was unnecessary, and nobody was asking me my opinion, which was great, because I didn't have one.

I was sitting in my position, in full costume and makeup, under the lights, while these two argued. Finally, I realized this was gonna take a while, and I got up to smoke a cigarette in the other room and get away from the heat of the lights. I fell asleep on some camera cases, woke up two hours later, and they were still arguing. Suddenly, they burst into the room and wanted to just pick up from where we left off, what was now two-and-a-half hours ago, without giving me anytime to get ready for the camera again. I had to shake myself from my stupor, fix my hair, makeup, and costume, and somehow focus my numbed brain on what we had been doing. I could have chosen to start arguing with them, but that would have gotten us all nowhere. An actor cannot be simply turned on and off like a light switch. Unfortunately, many inexperienced directors seem to forget that.

THE INVENTIVENESS OF GUERRILLA FILMMAKING

The absence of a big budget for a film should not represent a lack of creativity. In fact, some of the most exciting films have been shot for very little money. The restrictions caused by a low budget can inspire tremendous inventiveness in filmmakers, and the actor is very often part of that process. Because you are working with a small crew, you discuss things with one another and work things out together. Improvisations often arise as the solution to a scene that is not working. A suggestion from an actor about how to portray a certain aspect of his or her character often saves the day if it inspires the director's vision. The human element portrayed by the actors is perhaps low-budget film's best calling card.

It can be very exhilarating to be riding in a van, and the director spots something that he or she thinks is wonderful and, on the spur of the moment, decides, "Let's shoot that scene here instead of where we were going to shoot it." You all hop out, quickly decide where to take your places, and start doing the scene. It's wonderful. This kind of spontaneous unplanned shooting is called "shooting wild." Of course, if you haven't prepared yourself properly as an actor, it could be your worst nightmare, but most actors adore the challenge of the moment and find it exciting and fun. Shooting wild isn't really possible on a big-budget film, where everything has been carefully planned and organized. A director's style may utilize such techniques to give the film a certain look and feel, but they are not spontaneous decisions that jump at you in a moment's notice. A period of a spontaneous style of shooting is also planned in a big-budget movie.

THE SAG ACTOR

If you are already a member of Screen Actors Guild, you can still work on many no/low-budget and student films. The Guild has many contracts that allow members to work on these projects. Most film schools have an agreement with SAG, and you can work under the Student Film contract. Some of the other agreements are the Experimental, the Limited Exhibition, the Low-Budget, the Affirmative Action Low-Budget, and the Modified Low-Budget agreements. Each of these contracts is stipulated according to its production budgets and its potential distribution possibilities. A mixture of SAG and non-SAG actors is allowed, and the crews do not have to be union. The Modified Low-Budget Agreement, however, is very close to the full-scale contract. You can get all of the information about each contract from your local SAG office by asking for the Film Digest. This digest lists each contract in a simplified way that is easy to understand. If you are a Guild member, you can just pick one up. This information can also be found by doing a search for film contracts on the SAG Web site *(www.sag.com).*

These contracts have opened up the playing field of opportunities for professional actors to do more diverse work. It also has enabled filmmakers to use a higher quality of actor where their budgets might have prohibited them from doing so in the past. If someone has promised you one of these agreements, then it must be signed before you go before the camera.

Unfortunately, filmmakers, particularly on the lower-budget end, will sometimes lie to you to get you to work for less or no money. If you have an agent, he should look out for you and take care of your contractual commitments. Actors need respect and confidence to work properly, and having the feeling that you are being taken advantage of does not foster those feelings.

IMDb.COM

If you would like to do some research on any director who has asked you to work on his film, the easiest way is on the Internet. The best site is *www.imbd.com,* the Internet Movie Database. This site has actors, directors, writers, producers, and crew members on pages that list all of their credits internationally. It covers all aspects of the film industry, including television, for any film that has been released theatrically or is or was readily available for view by the public. This database also has biographies, trivia, gossip, chat rooms, and film news. Most people in the business use it all the time, for fun and for research. Once you start appearing in films, you will be listed there, too.

THE BIG-BUDGET MOVIE

I'm not really sure what the money value of a big-budget movie is anymore, since the price tags on films keep skyrocketing, but a good way to judge one is that it will have the basic SAG contract, a well-known director, and name actors or stars in the lead roles. Any movie with these components has to have a sizeable budget. If the film involves violence, special effects, or amazing stunts, the price tag goes up. To suspend a car from a helicopter that crashes into a wall, where both burst into flames, costs a lot of money and expertise to do. Fights that involve stunts are very time-consuming to shoot and require special stunt coordinators and skilled camera movements; this also costs a lot of money. Movies with sets that are expensive to create, like *Titanic, Age of Innocence,* or the *Star Wars* movies, come with a whole cadre of special needs and effects that send their budgets sailing through the roof.

If you work on a big-budget movie, there is one thing of which you can be sure—you will be treated very nicely while working. How nice it is to actually do the job will depend on your relationship to the director and your role, but all care will be taken to provide you with the amenities you need to be as comfortable as possible. First of all, you will be under the protection of the unions, with their meal regulations, rest periods, and time restrictions. If the filmmakers break any union rules, they must pay you penalties. There is overtime after eight hours of work. It may be the same grueling schedule of a low-budget film, but at day's end, you've been paid handsomely for your labor.

If you are shooting on location, you will have a comfortable, if not luxurious, hotel, per diem, and be driven to and from the set. The meals range from good to fabulous, depending on the caterer. There will be top-notch professionals doing every job on and off the set. Your hair will be done, your makeup designed, applied, and touched up. There will be a costume designer and a wardrobe crew. Your props will be arranged by the prop master. You will have a comfortable place to rest between shots, like a trailer or a segment of a honeycomb. A honeycomb is a long trailer with little, separate private compartments. Basically, all you have to do is show up and act.

It sounds wonderful, but as I said before, all films are the same, so even though the conditions vastly surpass those on a low-budget set, the basic dilemmas of filmmaking are still encountered; only now with the extra, added attraction of enormous pressure. When great deals of money are at stake, there are great expectations, and as an actor, you will certainly feel that a lot is expected of you. Famous people have personal relationships, too, and these can explode under the close quarters of the set. Stars, by the way, are also human beings; they have bad habits, they oversleep; they get angry and exhausted just like everyone else.

Big-budget movies are meticulously planned, and there are a lot of people at work to buffer bruised egos and fix problems that arise, but it's fascinating to see how the structure of filmmaking is so much the same at every level. The relationships of crew to talent (that's the actors), director to crew, director to actors, etc., is eerily similar, no matter what the budget or the style of the film. However, on a big-budget film, your involvement greatly advances your exposure and career.

If we go from the premise that the nature of filmmaking dictates that there are similarities in the procedures no matter what the budget, content, or style, then we can explore what some of those procedures are and how they affect the actor.

In the next chapter, I will lay out an actor's first day on the set of a medium- to big-budget film. It is a kind of template or example of the best-case scenario, the one that has been used for nearly a century around the world, wherever films are made. I guess it's because it seems to work best for everyone involved.

THE FIRST DAY ON THE SET

I must admit that I am always very excited about my first day on a set. I find it difficult to sleep the night before, my mind racing and adrenaline pumping through my veins in anticipation of the work to come. I never know what the work atmosphere will be. I'm like an athlete: prepared for action with my team, but having no way of knowing how the game is going to go—I just have to wait and take it play by play.

In this chapter, we will follow the path of the beginning of a hypothetical day on a moderate- to big-budget film, shot in 35mm, for an actor with a leading or supporting role. All variations on this theme, and there are many possible variations, come from this template. This is the norm.

BE PREPARED

Most movie work starts very early in the morning, so you can count on rising before dawn. Make sure that you have had plenty of rest in the days and nights preceding, because you might have trouble sleeping the night before. Do everything within your power to be in good mental and physical health. You know your body better than anyone else, so make sure it gets what it needs to function properly. The average day of shooting is twelve to fourteen hours; it will be strenuous work, so you should be in good condition.

Your acting instrument should be in good condition as well. Most of the work that you do must be done in your private, extended confrontation with the character—before you get in front of the camera. You're already well ahead of the game if you have been lucky enough to have had some form of rehearsal prior to shooting. But as I've mentioned in previous chapters, this will not always be the case; many times, your preparation has been left completely up to you.

There are a great many unknowns for the actor on the set, but the film production company has tried to schedule the days as efficiently as possible for all concerned. Sometimes, the difficulties of the actors are taken into consideration, but usually, the actor is not consulted in the planning process. The actor has little or no control in this area. There are things that are in your control and are expected of you when you start working; to some degree, they are the reasons that you were hired for this part in the first place.

YOUR LOOK

You have been hired because you have a certain look and energy. The production expects you to show up with that same look and energy. As a lead character, you have probably been styled and outfitted by the production beforehand. If you had straight, long, blonde hair when you were styled that they thought was great, you cannot show up for work with red hair and a perm. This would be a disaster for the production company. Sure, there are wigs, but they haven't planned one for you. You could hold up the entire production while they figure out what to do.

The same is true of your weight and physical condition. The stress before starting to shoot can do strange things to your body. Your best defense is to be aware of how you are physically reacting to the stress. If you do the relaxation and concentration during this time period, it will help you to focus.

THE INNER FOUNDATION

You should have gone through a thorough exploration of the emotional life of your character and how that character resonates in your acting technique. As I have mentioned before, a film character is continually evolving, right up until the final movie print is made. As the actor, you are expected to lay a sturdy foundation for the character, to support the possible demands that will be put on you to portray that character. This not only includes the scenes as depicted in the script, but any other ideas that may come up along the way. Once you're on the set, the director would like you to be able to perform anything that might be asked of you, believably and as the character. If you have done your preparation, you will be able to remain flexible to all demands put on you, while keeping an open mind.

THE SCRIPT

You are expected to have a thorough knowledge of the script, particularly your scenes. Your lines for the scheduled scenes that day must be memorized, and you should be prepared to quickly recall to memory any of the lines in the script in the event of a schedule change. Unlike a play rehearsal, a schedule change on a film set means that you're going "for real." If one of your scenes is replaced with another, you have to have worked on the rest of the script enough to act any part of it in an hour or two's notice.

Of course, you must be ready and on time for your pickup call. I would suggest waking up with enough time to do some kind of physical warm-up. I personally prefer a half-hour of not-too-strenuous yoga. This gets me stretched out, relaxed, and gets my breath in place. I will then do about ten to fifteen minutes of voice warm-ups, so my voice is protected and supported during the long day of shooting. Each person is different and should do whatever makes her most comfortable. I can tell you this, though: I am not a morning person—I naturally start to come alive in the evening—and it is for this reason that I always do warm-ups before an early pickup.

THE CALL SHEET

On the opposite page is the "call sheet," the shooting plan for the day. Every cast and crew member gets one. In the preproduction phase of the movie, all of the scenes have been given numbers in the consecutive order that they appear in the final shooting script. If there is a very long scene, it may be given more than one number, so that it can be broken up into workable sections. Each character in the movie has also been given a number. That is how the scenes, and the characters that are needed to play them, are identified on the large scheduling board in the production office. This board is the projected shooting schedule for the entire movie. It is not in the sequence of the shooting script; it is in the sequence that the production has deemed most efficient to shoot the movie. The schedule can change from day to day, due to a wide range of reasons. Each day, towards the end of the day, the production manager makes an assessment of what has been accomplished on the set that day and how to proceed with the next day's schedule. The logistics of the next day's shoot is handed out to the cast and crew on the call sheet.

How close a movie sticks to its production schedule varies in each case. The general rule is that everything takes much longer than expected. There are some directors who stay strictly on schedule, as planned, and never waver. Sidney Lumet is famous for this and says the call sheet is his bible. There are others who lose track of the time or just keep shooting until they are satisfied. Then, there are the millions of reasons that a film will go off schedule, reasons that are acts of God and reasons that are caused by human error and emotion. In most cases, each day is a new experience to be assessed and planned accordingly.

The call sheet I have made up is for a hypothetical movie called *Bucket of Blood,* by the fictitious director, Sarah Vision.

Call Sheet		
#1 General Information Director: Sarah Vision Asst. Dir. Robert Glad 917-242-3066	**Bucket of Blood**	Date: Mon. 4-01-02 Day 14 Crew Call: 8:00 A Shooting: 9:00 A

#2 The Scenes

	Scenes	Characters	Pages	Locations
Int. Joe's Bar-D *Zina tells Sammy off*	48	1, 3, 8, 11, 12	1 4/8	Hoople's Bar and Grill 48-36 Russel Street, Brooklyn, NY
Int. Joe's Bar-N *Typical Sat. night*	62	2, 3, 8, 11, 12	2 1/8	
Int. Joe's Bar-Backroom *Zina gets away*	63	2,3	5/8	
Ext. Side entrance-Dusk *Alina meets Zina*	64	1, 2	5/8	Russel Street outside of bar back entrance-Magic Hour-weather permitting

#3 The Cast

	Character	P/U	M/U	SET
1. Alice Vait	Alina	7:00A	7:30A	9:00 AM
2. Roam Kally	Zina	7:15A	7:30A	9:00 AM
3. Johnny Gee	Joe	8:00A	8:15A	9:00 AM
8. Barry Philco	Sammy	8:00A	8:15A	9:00 AM
11.Susan Mitch	Deanna	7:30A	8:00A	9:00 AM
12.Rocco Simi	Jo Jo	8:00A	8:15A	9:00 AM

4 Background and Props

	Props	Special Instructions:
Standins: 8:15		Steady Cam SC 48 SC 64 Weather permitting
30 bkgrnd: 7:30		Bkgrnd holding: 48-26 Russel St. Brooklyn, NY

#5 Crew Calls

Dir: 8:00 A	First AD: 8:00 A	DP: 8:00 A	Prod Asst.: 8:00 A	Electrics: 8:00 A	Sound: 8:00
ScriptS: 8:30	craft serv: 7:00	Grips: 8:00	makeup: 7:00	wardrobe: 7:30	Dailies: 8:30 PM

VEHICLES & OTHER: con't next pg.

#6 Advanced Schedule

JOE'S BAR LOCATION WRAPS WED. COMPLETE ALL SCENES BY WED!!!!!
4/03/02

SECTION ONE: GENERAL INFO
- It is the fourteenth day of shooting.
- The name and cell phone number of the assistant director; the person you would call in case of emergency.
- The crew is called for 8:00 AM on the set.
- Shooting should begin at 9:00 AM.

SECTION TWO: THE SCENES
- The set description tells us the slug lines of the scenes to be done that day. A very brief description of the action follows each scene.
- The scene numbers as they appear in the final shooting script and on the production planning board.
- The characters that are needed for these scenes, identified by their numbers.
- The amount of pages that the scene represents in the shooting script. A page of a shooting script is broken into eighths.
- The shooting location of the scenes that day.

On this call sheet, there are four scenes planned. Scenes 48, 62, and 63 are all interiors on the same location, the bar Hoople's. Scene 64 is an exterior shot with a weather-permitting flag. This scene is to be shot at sunset, in what is called "magic hour," when a special type of natural light exists just before and after the setting sun. It will only be shot if conditions are desirable. We know from the shooting script that scene 48 takes place a week or so before the consecutive time sequence of scenes 62, 63, and 64.

SECTION THREE: THE CAST
- The cast identified by number.
- The cast identified by the actor's name.
- The cast identified by the character's name.
- The time that they will be picked up by a driver.
- The time that they are due in the makeup department to begin their makeup.
- The time that they are due on the set, camera-ready for the first scene.

Before an actor can go before the camera, she must be made "camera-ready." Camera-ready means that the makeup, hair, and clothing of the character have been applied to the actor by the various departments responsible for them. The actor is ready to go before the camera. The normal sequence of events is pickup, makeup, wardrobe, and then on the set.

SECTION FOUR: BACKGROUND AND PROPS

- The time that the stand-ins for the lead actors are due on the set. The stand-in is your "light double," who stands in your place while the crew works, so that you can get ready to act in front of the camera. They do this while you are in makeup and wardrobe, and they also do it throughout the day after a camera/acting rehearsal on the set. The actors are called the first team, the stand-ins are called the second team.
- The reporting time of the background actors. These are the extras in the movie. In this movie, they are the people in the bar. Since there will be a busy Saturday night scene, there are thirty called for that day.
- All special props that are needed by the lead actors.
- The special instructions tell us that a Steadicam camera will be used for scene 48 and the time of sunset because scene 64 takes place at magic hour. It also tells us where the background actors will stay when they are not needed on the set. This is called the "holding area."

SECTION FIVE: CREW CALLS

- The times that each important crew member or department is due to start work on the set.
- The organization of the drivers and vehicles that will pick up the cast and crew.
- A note that dailies (the rushes) will be shown at 8:30 PM. Only select members of the crew watch the dailies with the director; they know who they are.

SECTION SIX: ADVANCE SCHEDULE

The projected schedule for the next few days. In this case, whatever scenes are remaining for Joe's Bar will have to be completed by Wednesday. Hoople's, the real bar that serves as the location for Joe's, will have to be vacated by Wednesday night for its usual weekend business. That means the crew will have to clear everything out of that location and restore it to its normal owners. When a production has completed shooting and has vacated a location, they say the location has been "wrapped." Wrapped, in film lingo, means ended, completed, done with, finished.

Every cast and crew member who is to report that day will receive the call sheet the night before. If it is your first day on the set, a production assistant will call you a day or so before and let you know what the schedule on the call sheet is. The actual call sheet is not decided upon and printed up until the latter part of the previous day's shooting, when they can be more certain of what they have accomplished and if they will be able to proceed as planned. For an actor, this can mean a lot of starts and stops. They may tell you on Tuesday that they need you on Thursday for such and such a scene, only to call you on Wednesday evening to say the whole thing has been pushed back to next week, and they will now need you starting on Monday. This can cause a lot of anxiety. It's a good time to go back to the chair and do those relaxation exercises to focus on what's important, that you do the best job you're able to do in front of the camera, and not to get involved with the anxiety of your anticipation. That's just the way it is in the movie business. It's always hurry up and wait.

THE ACTOR AND THE CALL SHEET

Let's assume that you are playing Zina, a lead role in this movie, and your name is Roam Kally. From the information on the call sheet, you know what scenes you are shooting today and the order in which they will be shot. You're lucky today, because scenes 62, 63, and 64 will be shot in sequence, in the order that they appear in the shooting script. This is always best for the actor, for obvious reasons. You can also tell that everything will be shot on the same location, which is also good for the actor, because you can "bunker in" and feel some sort of reality from the surroundings; there will be a continuity of place, which is always comforting. You also know that your character will be wrapped by 8:30 PM because the dailies are being shown, and key crew members, along with the director, will have to view them. There's one more comforting bit of news in this: You know that if you are home by 8:30 PM, your next day's pickup call cannot be earlier than 8:30 AM, because of a twelve-hour turnaround law. You must have twelve hours off between drop-off and pickup. So, all in all, it should be a very good day. Of course, everything could change in an instant for reasons beyond your control, but that's part of the fun.

The last scene of the day, scene 64, has a weather-permitting note indicated on the sheet. That means that there is a certain type of light or sky that the director has in mind for this scene. Since weather is beyond anyone's control, the scene is up in the air until the very last moment. That moment will be around the hour of sunset, and the decision to shoot or not to shoot will be made at that time. Everyone assumes until the final second that it's going to be a go.

I once worked on a Woody Allen movie set in the 1920s with a huge cast. We had a 5:30 AM makeup call, which meant rising at 3:30 AM for me. There was a series of exterior shots that he wanted to do with a crowd on the beach and a certain type of cloud formation in the sky over the ocean. We waited four days for those clouds. Each day, we would arrive, get camera-ready, and wait. At the end of the day, we were wrapped and told to come back tomorrow. On the fourth day, they scrapped the scenes altogether. If he couldn't get what he wanted, he didn't want it at all, and it was becoming too expensive to wait any longer. No one complained; we all just took it in stride.

Back to *Bucket of Blood*. Since you are a lead character, you have been styled and fitted for makeup and wardrobe a week or so before your first day of shooting. On the call sheet, you see that your pickup time is 7:15 AM. You will be brought directly to the set, where you will have a trailer or a honeycomb compartment of your own. An actress can count on an hour or two of allotted time for ordinary makeup, hair, and costume; for men, it's usually much shorter. You will probably have time to make a quick stop at craft services (the table or truck with coffee, donuts, bagels, etc., which supplies snacks and beverages for cast and crew in between the meal periods) to grab a cup of coffee that you can take with you when you report to the makeup trailer.

THE MAKEUP DEPARTMENT

The makeup department on a major motion picture is nothing to be taken lightly. It is the first department of many that the actor comes in contact with on a film set. It is comprised of the following jobs:

KEY MAKEUP ARTIST

This person has the last word on designing the look for all the characters on the film. She is an important crew member who is privy to the way each character is supposed to look for each appearance in front of the camera. She designs the makeup and hair and oversees any special effects, wounds, alien protrusions, prostheses, etc. Makeup is very important to maintaining the time continuity of the picture and the key makeup artist is like the foreman of a crew who makes sure that once the makeup is designed, the continuity is maintained and the style of the movie is serviced. The key makeup artist is in charge of:

ASSISTANT MAKEUP ARTISTS

These are the assistants to the key makeup artist who apply the designed makeup on the actors. One of them will be on set to do touch-ups between takes. There might be one or two of them, or there could be a small army of them, depending on the size of the cast for any particular day.

HAIRSTYLIST

This person designs the hairstyles and is responsible for the cutting, coloring, and styling of the hair, wigs, moustaches, etc., for all the actors. There are usually one or two assistants as well, and one of them will also be on the set at all times to do touch-ups between takes.

BODY MAKEUP ARTIST

The body makeup artist takes care of all makeup that is applied from the neck down. If any flesh is showing, bare arms, bare back, or legs, these parts get an application of body makeup; normal, naked flesh doesn't photograph well under intense lights. Those luminous skin tones that you see in the movies are the result of the body makeup artist's meticulous work. They also get to do the mud, dirt, blood, etc.

SPECIAL EFFECTS PERSON

Depending on the needs of the script or the genre of the film, this person might design and apply the complex mechanisms required for special effects makeup. It is an exciting and expanding field in the movie industry, as more and more complex effects become possible. On our imaginary movie, there is no special effects person needed.

These artists will have an order of application and construction in mind for your makeup and hair; you just allow them to do whatever they need to do. In order to get all the actors ready for their 9:00 AM set call, they need to work quickly and efficiently. However, as they put together the physical appearance of the character, they will chat and joke and keep a fairly jovial atmosphere going. They usually adhere to Napoleon's famous statement to his valets: "Dress me slowly; I'm in a hurry."

I personally have always looked forward to the artists in the makeup trailer. It's usually a very good time. They can relax an actor in a way that lets the character sneak in almost unbeknownst to herself. When they're done with you, you have begun to transform into someone else, the character. Then, they'll send you over to the wardrobe trailer to get dressed.

THE COSTUME DEPARTMENT

The costume department is comprised of the following:

COSTUME DESIGNER

You probably met the costume designer while you were being outfitted for the character. This person, like the key makeup artist, is responsible for all of the clothing that the actors wear in the film. Most of his work is done off set, designing.

WARDROBE SUPERVISOR AND ASSISTANTS

The people the actors come in contact with are the wardrobe supervisor and his assistants. These are the people who are in charge of organizing and maintaining the wardrobe, as well as dressing the actors on the set. A member of the wardrobe supervisor's crew will be available on the set at all times to make sure that the costumes maintain continuity for picture.

For some reason, wardrobe always seems to be a much more somber affair in comparison to the makeup trailer. Perhaps it's because it's where people get naked and dressed, and it requires a setting of decorum.

From your call sheet, you know that scene 48 is the first scene up, and you will be styled and made up for that scene. The following scenes, 62, 63, and 64, take place at a later time. You will have a makeup and costume change for those scenes. In fact, many of the lead actors will have changes. When scene 48 has completed filming, you will be sent back to the makeup and wardrobe trailers to get camera-ready for scenes 62, 63, and 64. The call sheet tells you that a Steadicam is going to be used for scene 62. A Steadicam is a camera that is strapped onto the operator and can move freely, and in focus, with its operator. There are thirty background actors for this scene as well. More than likely, the background actors will be placed on the set, told what to do, and much of their business will be shot while you and the other lead actors are going through your change.

When you are done changing, you will report back to the set and rehearse the next scene, in this case, scene 62. The background actors will be incorporated into the shots, and they will rehearse with you. The background actors will stay on the set, while you might have a chance to take a break (usually about twenty minutes to half an hour). Your light double will be standing in for you as you prepare to act before the camera. Somewhere along the way, you've been given a half-hour to eat breakfast, and lunch should be at least six hours into shooting. You can see why it's a good idea to have a character log that you can refer to, to help you remember what it was you wanted to do for each scene in the first place.

Movies are a portable world of trailers. Even on the lots of the studios, many of the offices and departments are in trailers. This way, whether the production is in a studio or on location, the various departments are already set up in their trailers, ready to go to wherever the shoot is. If you are a gypsy at heart, this is a very appealing factor.

THE ACTOR AND THE CREW

During your time in the makeup or wardrobe trailers, you may encounter agitated young people with walkie-talkies and hurried looks on their faces. They will come into the trailer and bark into the walkie-talkie, bark at those at work, and probably bark at you, too. These are the production assistants, or PAs, as they are commonly called, a group of people who perform a variety of tasks on the production. The ones the actors come in contact with are the messenger/escorts. They deliver information to whomever needs it: "The director wants you on set as soon as you're ready," "The costume designer is coming and wants the actor playing Jojo to report to wardrobe first thing for a fitting," "We need the actors on the set ASAP," etc. They also escort the actors from one place to another. They rarely introduce or identify themselves to you. Their demeanor can be upsetting to the organized calm of the makeup and wardrobe process.

The PAs represent the actor's first encounter with the crew members who are working on the movie set. They are the front runners on the dividing line between cast and crew. The crew's work is labor-intensive, and each crew member knows where he stands in the hierarchy of his department and the production as a whole. Crew members work diligently to prepare the space into which the actors step to work. Everything is done for the picture. There is a definite dividing line between those who work in front of the camera and those who work behind it. This seems to exist on all movies, no matter their style, budget, or director.

When you are ready to go to the set, the crew will be working around you. To give you a clearer understanding of what those you see around you are actually doing, here is a list of some of the departments, their crew members, and what their responsibilities are:

THE DIRECTING UNIT

The director of the movie is the head of the directing unit. I think that we are all familiar with who the director is; how she goes about doing the job is a matter of style. Basically, the director is responsible for taking the script and putting it into pictures with sound. The director is involved with all of the creative decisions on the film, from pre- through postproduction. To help her do this job are:

First Assistant Director

This person works very closely with the director and the production manager. The responsibilities include making sure the shoot runs smoothly, navigating the background actors, and assisting in giving direction to the actors. On the set, this person is referred to as first AD. First ADs also oversee a lot of paperwork, like the call sheet.

Second Assistant Director

The second AD assists the director and first AD, mainly with logistics and paperwork.

Dialogue Coach

In the event that the film requires certain types of speech or accents, a dialogue coach will be on the set to oversee the consistency of the spoken text.

CINEMATOGRAPHY

This is the camera crew, led by the director of photography.

Director of Photography

The director of photography, or DP, is responsible for all moving pictures in the film. The DP chooses the equipment and labs that will be used to shoot the picture, as well as the rest of the camera crew. The DP is as important to the film as the director is. The two must work well together for the picture to be successful.

Camera Operator

The person who operates the camera that is taking the picture. Most DPs have operators that they work with. Sometimes, the DP will operate the camera himself on certain scenes. On the lower end of filmmaking, the DP is also the camera operator.

First Camera Assistant

This person assists the operator by pulling focus, measuring the distance for the focus, and making sure that the gate is clean. This is the person who will come towards you with a tape measure and give you marks. If there is a mark that you are supposed to hit for the camera, you must do it accurately and without looking like you're doing it.

Second Camera Assistant
The loader. This assistant cleans and maintains the camera and its parts, as well as loading and unloading the film.

ELECTRICAL DEPARTMENT
The electrical department works under the director of photography. On a big-budget film, particularly if there are large spaces being lit and photographed, this could be a big crew.

Gaffer
The chief electrician is called the gaffer and is in charge of the lighting needed by the DP to get the picture that is desired.

Best Boy
The best boy is the assistant to the gaffer and takes care of the equipment. I've never seen a woman do this job. I'm sure that female best boys exist, but I am not sure if they would be called best girls. My guess is probably not.

Electricians
Responsible for rigging and operating the lights. On a big-budget film, there could be a lot of electricians.

GRIP DEPARTMENT
Grips are carpenters and construction workers. They build and operate the things that hold the lights and move the camera.

Key Grip
The key grip oversees these workers and answers to the director and the director of photography.

Dolly Grip
The dolly is a cart on wheels on which the camera is placed to move it while shooting. It is often on tracks to ensure a smooth ride. The dolly grip lays the tracks and operates this cart. The dolly grip is also responsible for the cranes that move the camera.

Grips
These are the people who swing the tools that build the things needed to fulfill the key grip's instructions.

THE SOUND DEPARTMENT

As the name implies, the sound department is responsible for the sound of the movie. This includes the recording of the dialogue of the actors. A lot of the sound departments' work takes place off set and in postproduction, but the crew members on the set are:

Production Sound Mixer

This person is usually somewhere out of the way of the camera and will be wearing headphones and sitting at a cart with a sound mixing board. He records and mixes the levels of all the sound on the set needed for the picture.

Boom Operator

This person is always very close to the actors if a boom is being used. The boom is a type of microphone that is held at the end of a long pole. The problem that the boom operator faces, besides exhausted arms, is holding the boom close enough to the actors for the speech and sounds to be recorded, but out of the frame of the picture. It also cannot cast a shadow anywhere in the frame. I've had boom operators practically laying between my legs as I acted, because it was the only place they could go to ensure that their job be done.

PROPS DEPARTMENT
Property Master

The property master is responsible for all the props called for in the script. These include all the things that are handled by the actors.

Assistants

The assistants to the property master care for and place all the props that an actor uses in the film. The actors only touch them when they are working. After each take, the property assistants will replace the props.

THE SCRIPT SUPERVISOR

This is a very important job on any production. This person is responsible for taking detailed notes of each take during the production. The position is often referred to as Continuity. Script supervisors record the scene, the take number, the camera position, and what lens was used. They also record changes in the dialogue and the actions of the actors. The script supervisor notes every single thing that you do or say, when you picked up a glass, if you brushed your hair out of your eyes, and what small pauses or word changes you have incorporated into the text. The script supervisor's vital observations are reported back to the actor during the various coverage takes. The script supervisor is on set during shooting at all times. Never disagree with her, even if you are sure you're right. This job has been dominated by women in the industry from the very beginning; they still dominate this field. That is why the position is often called the "script girl."

TALENT

The actors or any performer in front of the camera, even animals, are referred to as "talent." I'm not sure if the term is sarcastic or not; I'll really have to try and find out where it started.

There are a lot of people on a set, as you can tell from the previous list, who are all more or less in fairly close proximity to your work area. Many of them will be staring directly at you as you work, some to judge your acting performance, some to watch that your appearance remains appropriate for the scene, others to watch for unwanted shadows, and still others to make sure that as you move, you stay within the frame and in the correct focus for that shot. Each will have something to say to you; each is equally important. Your actual playing time at any given moment is usually just a few minutes. Most of the time is spent preparing everything for those few minutes when the camera is actually rolling.

The need and usage of the relaxation, the concentration, and the value of the small subtle gestures of the face will become very clear to you when you are called to the set for your first camera blocking rehearsal of the first scene of the day. Whatever you have prepared for this scene must be incorporated into the direction of the director. You've got to feel yourself out on your first day. You must be attentive to the style and desires of the director and the crew around you. You have to feel out the dynamic and how the director wants you to behave. Whatever he wants, whatever rhythm is set, whatever joke or seriousness prevails, you must find a way to fit in and follow the lead of the director. Even if you disagree with creative decisions or questions of taste, you have to respect his authority and do it his way. It's the only way you will be able to work.

In an interview in a special movie edition of *los angeles* magazine, Jodie Foster said, " I really believe that the actor's job is to serve the director . . . even if by week one you realize he doesn't know what he wants . . . or you don't like his style, you still have to serve him. . . . [T]he director is the visionary of the movie, they get to have the party the way they want it." You won't know how the director likes his party until you start working on the set with him. Just remember, you have been invited to this party, and as a guest of honor, you're expected to behave yourself appropriately. Don't throw your energy around haphazardly; you will need it for the day ahead. In the next chapter, I will describe some of the possible camera setups and ways that a scene could be shot, to give you a better idea of what to expect.

HOT SET: THE CLASSIC CAMERA SETUPS

Walking onto the set to begin working on a scene is like walking into a house that is in the process of being built. Invariably, there's the sound of drills and the clinking of metal on metal. A peculiar, warm smell emanates from the lights, and the hum of busy conversation prevails, interrupted by a barked order or an abrupt question. The brightest spot in the room is where you are headed. The place that is the focus of everyone's attention, where the camera lens is pointed; that's the place that you will be stepping into: the hot set.

The playing area in an interior location is usually a small part of a larger space; the crew and equipment take up most of the room. Once on the set, the first AD or the director will bring you to your position. When the first shot is nearly ready from the crew's point of view, when everything has been basically set in place, the actors step into the scene to begin the rehearsal. If you haven't had any previous rehearsals, you might be meeting your fellow actors for the first time. Everyone has different methods of working and dealing with the stress that comes with the anticipation of performance, so be cordial and easygoing. It's very important to stay calm and conserve your energy. Don't worry about acting or how you will do; stay in the moment. This moment is about becoming accustomed to your surroundings and meeting new people.

COVERAGE

I think it's helpful to know how film scenes are covered by the different camera shots in order to understand the film-set rehearsal. The different camera angles and movements are called shots or setups (these involve moving the camera). The different shots comprise the way the camera has photographed a particular scene. This is called "coverage," because the scene has been covered from different angles and perspectives to tell its story. The general rule is to start with the longest and widest shots and work your way down to the smaller, closer ones. The director and DP make these decisions. Since the actor is not consulted, you never know what the coverage of a particular scene will be until you're on the set and are told what to do. Here's a list of some of the possible shots used in covering a scene.

- Master shot—the whole scene shot from beginning to end in a wide camera angle. This would include all of the action, blocking, and dialogue in the scene. If the scene is very long, then a large portion will be shot.

- Establishing shot—this is also done from a wider angle, usually to establish the relationship of a character or characters to their surroundings.

- Two shot—two characters in the same frame.

- Medium shot—the character is shown in the frame from the waist up. Most dialogue is photographed in this manner.

- Over-the-shoulder—somewhere between a medium shot and a close-up. One character's back is to the camera, with just part of the shoulder and head in the foreground of the frame as they face the other character, whose full face is shown. Most scenes with dialogue between two characters are covered in this manner.

- Close-up—the character from the neck up or just the face in the frame.

- Extreme close-up—this is a very close shot, with only room for part of the face in the camera frame.

- Macro—only one aspect of the face in the frame, like one eye or a mole on the corner of the lip. A new lens has been invented that allows a shot to begin in macro and zoom out to a wide panoramic view of the surroundings.

- P.O.V.—stands for point of view. This is shot from a character's perspective and shows the viewer what the character sees.

- Insert—this is usually a shot of an object at close range, like handwriting or picking up a glass, which is inserted into the scene during editing. Often the second team will shoot these shots, instead of the principal actors.

- Zoom—the camera is stationary as the lens moves in closer.

- Dolly shot—the camera moves on a dolly cart.

- Pan—the camera moves from left to right or right to left.

- Tilt—the camera moves up to down or down to up.

Moving the actual camera position requires a lot of time and preparation. For this reason, after the master shot has been photographed, the scene will be covered from one position at a time. Directors like to have a lot of coverage for their scenes, because it gives them more editing choices in postproduction. The same scene might be repeated over and over again from each camera position, with closer shots done along the way.

THE FIRST REHEARSAL

Let's suppose that you are the right actor for this job, and, therefore, you have all the emotional and technical ammunition to do whatever is asked of you. The first rehearsal is going to be a blocking rehearsal for the actors. The rest of the key crew members will be watching the rehearsal to anticipate the coming demands on their departments once it is decided how to shoot the scene. Directors have varying degrees of preconceived ideas about how to film a scene. They have discussed it with their key crew members and probably have a planned shot list of some kind; however, it isn't until the live bodies of the actors are on the set, starting to bring the characters to life, that all final decisions are made.

Hitchcock was an excellent draftsman and had all of his films completely planned visually before he started production. The entire film was carefully created in his head. He said that filming was the most boring part for him, because, in his mind, the film was already finished; he only had to photograph it. Most directors do not fall into this category of preparedness. They enjoy the creative, spontaneous aspect of discovering what the actor has to bring to the scene. An actor friend of mine who was working with a very famous director on a big-budget film told me this story: When my friend asked the director what he wanted from a scene, the director looked at him blankly and said, "How the hell do I know, that's what I hired you for!"

Of course, these two examples represent the extremes; the norm falls somewhere in between. And this, in my opinion, is the exciting part of acting in film. The cast comes on the set, the set has been dressed and prepared and lit. Now the actors are given a range of movement and an environment to work within and asked to run through the scene. Within the scope of the playing area you are often given free reign to move, to act, and to react as you see fit. The director watches and adjusts your movements and gives you notes. You take the adjustments that you understand and inquire, simply, about the ones you don't. You do the scene again. If it is an emotional scene, you shouldn't act fully: You must have your engine going, but keep your foot off the gas; the camera isn't rolling yet. It is at this point that many of the actor's ideas will be incorporated into the shot construction of the scene. If what the actors have offered in terms of movement and interpretation fits into the telling of the story, it will be accepted. Every improvisational skill, every exercise where you have struggled to stay in the moment, and every minute you have spent developing your inner sensorial response to outer stimuli will come in handy now. You are constructing the imaginary reality of the character's life in the first blocking rehearsal. You must be connected to what you are doing at this moment, because it will become the master shot from which all other shots for this scene will be matched.

After the director and DP have conferred on how to shoot the scene, they will set the blocking by giving you marks that you must hit. These marks are little pieces of tape, unseen by the camera, that you have to hit at given moments in the scene. You must put yourself through the paces of hitting your marks and find a way of hitting them without looking at them. It is an essential aspect of working in front of the camera. If you aren't used to doing this, it can feel very constricting and false. Just accept it as part of the job, do it as best you can, don't panic, and justify any movement within your acting logic.

Now that the blocking of the master shot has been decided upon, some lighting adjustments will have to be made, the sound crew will figure out what to do with their microphones, and you should be ready to shoot. Hopefully, all of the adjustments will only take a short time. If they require a lot of time, the second team will be called in to stand in your place, while the first team, the cast, is given time to assimilate what the blocking rehearsal has brought out in the scene and get their preparation ready to act it in front of the camera. The second team has been watching your movements from the sidelines and will copy them for the lighting and sound crews while they do their jobs. This could be a twenty-minute break, or it could be an hour or more; it depends on the preparedness of the director and the efficiency of the crew.

One of the ways I occupy my waiting time on my first day of shooting is the ten-minute game. If they tell me it will be ten minutes to shooting (ten seems to be everyone's favorite number), I check to see what time it is. Then, when we actually start shooting, I'll check again. It is never ten minutes; it's usually twenty or forty-five minutes. My game is to try and decipher on the first day what they mean when they say "ten minutes." When they say ten minutes, do they really mean an hour? I have been on low-budget films where ten minutes was consistently two hours. That was a drag.

SHOOTING THE MASTER

When it's finally time to shoot the master shot, the first AD will call in the first team, the cast, and ask for quiet on the set. The first camera assistant will ask you to hit certain marks while the light and distance is measured. There will be light meters and tape measures coming toward your face and body. The makeup assistant will be looking carefully at every corner and crevice of your face, wardrobe will be adjusting your dress, and the hair-stylist will be arranging and touching your hair. You should be concentrated on the instructions of the camera crew, who are making sure that what they have planned to do will actually work now that you are in the frame. Be aware of the lights and how they hit your face and how the specific movements that you have been given will affect the character's behavior. Remember that if you move outside of the camera frame, you will not be photographed; it doesn't matter how great you act if no one can see it.

You will walk through a tech rehearsal for camera and lights, to make sure that you understand your movements and then someone will say, okay, we're ready for picture. The crew will be asked to clear the frame—that means that all crew members and their tools and paraphernalia must exit the playing area where the actors are in position. The director will check with the DP that camera is ready for picture. Then, the atmosphere completely changes.

Before the camera rolls, the same procedure takes place each time.

- First AD: "Quiet on the set." Absolute silence immediately takes hold.

- Sound recorder: "Speed." The audio is running.

- Camera operator: "Rolling." The camera is filming.

- Camera assistant takes the clapper and puts it in front of the beginning position of the camera and slates (identifies) the shot. He claps the clapper.

- Director calls for "Action"; that's the actor's cue to begin.

- The scene is acted out as rehearsed and shot, until the director calls "Cut."

No matter what type of shot you're doing, the above procedure will take place. This procedure creates an atmosphere and work environment that has consistent rules for the actors:

- The actors' starting position is stationary and quiet. Actors do not make sounds or move during the steps before the call for "Action."

- When "Action" is called, the moment starts immediately; there's no warming up into it. It happens right then, on a dime.

- Always stay within the concentration of the scene, and keep acting even if you have made a mistake.

- Stay still when you have come to the end position of the scene, but keep acting until the director calls "Cut." If you don't know what to do, just keep investigating the moment that you are in, keep thinking and breathing; never stop until you hear "Cut."

- Never stop or look to the director if you've done something wrong; just keep going.

- Never look directly into the camera lens, unless specifically told to do so.

- If you are asked to do something, like lean forward for a certain line, wait two beats before you say something, or to look at a certain point at a specific time, just do it, even if it makes no sense to you and you don't know why. There are many technical concerns for camera continuity that you don't need to understand. As an actor, part of your job is to aesthetically make sense of whatever is being asked of you. Basically, whatever it is, *make it work.*

The master will only be shot two or three times. Each time the director yells "Cut," everyone stops what he or she is doing, and a short discussion of the technical merits of the scene follows. If they need to do it again, the first AD will say, "Back to one," or "Starting positions, we're going again." This means you are shooting exactly the same thing over again, adding whatever adjustments you have been given. The director may or may not pay any attention to the actors at this point. If she doesn't say anything, then assume what you are doing is right. When both the camera operator and the director are satisfied that they have what they need from the master, they will move on to the next shot.

SHOOTING THE REST OF THE SCENE

I know that when I act, I'm always trying to improve what I have just done; I want to go deeper or communicate better. I find new insight into the scene, or the relationship, or even just one single moment each time I repeat a scene or a segment of the scene. The repetitious nature of acting lends itself to using the discovery process, in order not to go stale with each repetition. The challenge is to re-create new and afresh with each repetition. When you're acting in a film, you really have the opportunity to explore the possibilities of your imagination and its ability to create a new, crystal clear moment that reveals character with each try. Each time you do a scene, whether you are given a direction or not, your inner desire should always be to do your best, even to best your best. Always work at making the scene fuller and more interesting with each take.

Let's suppose that the master that was just shot was from the first scene on the call sheet of the hypothetical movie from the previous chapter.

SC. 48 – INT. JOE'S BAR – DAY

The description on the call sheet simply says, Zina tells Sammy off, and it's one-and-two-eighths pages, which is exactly how long it is in the script. If this scene were taking place on stage, it would last about two minutes, which is more than it will last in the finished movie, though it will take half the day to shoot.

You are the actress playing the role of Zina. In your script, you come into the bar with your mother to prepare for Saturday night. Joe, your brother, is behind the bar, and a regular named Sammy makes a couple of wisecracks at you. You tell him off, and he leaves the bar. You know your lines. In the rehearsal and shooting of the master, everything that wasn't clear before has become clear. You felt fairly confident that what you did in the two takes of the master shot was good.

I have made up a possible shot list for the way the director might proceed with covering the rest of the scene to give you an idea how many times you will repeat this scene or parts of it. You will quickly see that if you want to go deeper into the character, and you should go deeper, you will have ample opportunity.

SHOT LIST FOR SCENE 48

All shots are with the camera pointing towards the bar over the backs of the customers. Each shot will be rehearsed separately, with lighting and sound adjustments made for each shot. The makeup and hairstylist will do touch-ups along the way as well. Once the master has been lit and shot, the rehearsal and lighting time for each new setup is usually quite short—that is, of course, if all goes smoothly and there aren't any real technical problems. Each shot will be repeated three to six times, but that's a conservative estimate. Six or more takes would not be too unusual on a big-budget movie.

- Master—wide angle of the entire scene. Joe is tending bar, chatting with a few regulars. Sammy sits at his usual perch at the end of the bar. Joe's mother, Alina, comes in with the bank for the night shift. Zina, his sister, comes in to do the liquor count.

Dialogue between Joe, Zina, and Sammy. Sammy hits on Zina, per usual, and she finally tells him off. The regulars react. Alina just goes about her business. This is the whole scene from beginning to end without a break.

- Establishing shot—Zina as she stands in the doorway and comes into the bar. The camera will start with just a stationary shot of Zina in the doorway. Here you would have to know where you are coming from, even if the script hasn't given you that information, and how you feel about coming into the bar.

- Pan—follows Zina into the bar and becomes the two shot.

- Two shot—Zina and Joe. Both go about their business, until Sammy chirps in with his hit on Zina. The pan and the two shot will be combined into one camera move, and the entire scene with all the dialogue will be included. The camera will focus on the upper part of Zina and Joe's bodies. All of the movement must match the master shot, but the emphasis here is on Zina and Joe's interaction with one another and their relationship.

- Over-the-shoulder—over Sammy's shoulder, looking towards Zina. The entire scene will be repeated in this over-the-shoulder shot, with Zina and her dialogue being the focus. This is a good opportunity to really show and explore the relationship that Zina has with Sammy and how she feels about what he's saying. The continuity again will have to match the master and the previous two shot.

- Close-up—on Zina. Her dialogue, starting with Joe, then between her and Sammy. Includes her reaction to him leaving the bar. In this close-up, Zina will remain stationary and do all of her dialogue. Joe and Sammy will be off camera, feeding Zina their lines. If at all possible, you will be able to look directly at them, but more than likely, you will be given dots as your sightlines for Joe and Sammy, and their voices will be coming from somewhere else. You will do the same for them—feed them your lines from an off-camera position—when they do their close-ups.

- Medium shot—Sammy cheats out towards camera, gets disgusted, and leaves. Here, we will see Sammy sitting at the bar with his body angled enough towards the camera that we can see his face, but it still looks like he is facing Zina. Zina will be in this shot in the background. There is no scripted dialogue here, though some may be ad libbed; it's just Sammy's reaction and his exit.

It is quite possible that at this point the camera will be turned around to face the other side of room. If this is going to occur it will take a long time to set up. There will be a break for the cast, while the crew completes the turnaround. The camera is moved to behind the bar for the following scenes:

- Establishing shot—customers interacting with Joe, the usual. Here the actors playing the regulars ad-lib dialogue and actions that will match their actions in the master.

- Medium shot—Sammy sees Zina enter and follows her every move. This shot has no dialogue for a long time. It's all Sammy's reaction to Zina. Zina, however, will not be there, because the camera and crew are now behind the bar. The actor playing Sammy will have to create Zina and follow her movements in his imaginary reality. This shot will end after Sammy's first line.

- Close-up—Sammy's dialogue with Zina. Zina and Joe will feed Sammy their lines off camera, more than likely crouched somewhere between the camera assistant and a lighting stand.

- Three shot—three regulars react to Zina's outburst. These are three guys sitting at the end of the bar who are witness to the whole scene. They will have to act for the camera as if they were watching the scene between Zina and Sammy. Their movements will have to match the master.

- Close-up—Deanna's reaction to the scene. Deanna, one of the regulars at the bar, gets her own reaction shot in close-up.

There are many different possibilities other than the above shot list; it's just a hypothetical example of what the sequence of events might be. If you are playing one of the lead roles, you will be working a lot in this scene, and you will need a sturdy foundation upon which to draw. All the preparation work discussed earlier might be needed, including sensory work for the place and perhaps substitution for the relationships. Every choice that you make must be brought to life through a thorough technique of relaxation and concentration. You will need to be energy efficient, because after all, it's only time to break for lunch. Afterwards the rest of the day's planned shooting schedule will continue. You can only find out how you do all this, appropriately for your particular talent, through experience, where you learn by trial and error.

There is a tremendous focus on detail in filmmaking and that includes the work of the actor. You have to have focused on the investigation of the possibilities of the character within yourself in order to have enough to offer the camera. If the camera is coming in closer and closer to you and your character, then there must be something to warrant the attention to such intimacy. If you haven't layered the character sufficiently in your preparations, it will appear one-dimensional or flat and uninteresting as the camera moves in nearer. If there's nothing new to photograph to illuminate the story, why bring the face of the character into a full frame in the first place?

WHAT TO DO WITH THE WRONG PREPARATION

Sometimes you can be very well-prepared for a scene, or so you think, and when you are confronted with what the director and crew have in mind, you find that your own expectation of the situation is completely different from theirs.

Movies are a media of pre-visualization. They are seen within the mind like a dream and then transposed onto the frame. Actors pre-visualize when they read a script or work on the character. This pre-visualization happens automatically and affects how you proceed with your preparation of the character. The medium, as it exists in script form, is constructed to make pre-visualization a must. However, it is not the vision of the actor that is transposed to the frame; it is the vision of the director and the director of photography. So how do you deal with the rejection of your vision or the rash clash that happens within you when what you thought was going to happen doesn't? When what you saw in your mind's eye has nothing to do with what is being presented to you?

Let's take for an example one of the other scenes from the call sheet, scene 63. This is a scene that is identified by a slug line and an action description only, there is no dialogue. In the script, scene 63 read as follows:

SC. 63 — INT. JOE'S BAR — BACKROOM — NIGHT
Zina, exhausted and fed up, steals away alone to gather her thoughts.

In your mind's eye, when you first read the script, you saw the backroom in this scene as being a small, closet-sized office. You imagined that because the scene was given such a short description in the script that it would be quick and simple in the shooting. When you see the location where scene 63 is to be shot, it is a large room adjoining the bar where parties are held. It has been carefully dressed as an almost ghostly ballroom in shabby demise. Chandeliers have been hung, and the whole atmosphere is rich with fantasy and promise. The actions that are possible in this elaborate playing area wouldn't be possible in the one you imagined in your head. At first you seem to go into a kind of shock; it's just so different from what you expected, and you don't know what to do. Matters are made worse when the director turns to you and says, "So, whadiya' think, it's beautiful, isn't it? How should we shoot this? Any ideas?" How do you adjust your technique and interpretation to the realities of the location and this sudden freedom that's been thrust upon you?

For starters, you don't have to do anything. Just be in the moment, and take in the space.

You take the thoughts and feelings of you, the actor, and make them the thoughts and feelings of the character in this situation. You use the here and now. You could, for example, take the feeling of having been in a small, cramped space, and now you are free to explore this large, interesting new place that you have never seen before. As the actor, you are confronted by a set that doesn't look as you thought it would; as the character, you are searching for something new. Seize this opportunity. If you put the two together and play the moment, the dilemma of the actor is transformed into the dilemma of the character. If you have left yourself alone while preparing, if you have allowed your imagination free reign to operate within the confines of the script, then it will be there for you now. Anyway, you are not alone in this endeavor; there is a whole crew of professionals who are carefully watching you, including your director. Everyone is waiting to see what you breathe into this space to make it come alive in the story. The actor only needs to reach for a spark of the imagination and allow it to flow, the others will formalize it into pictures and actions.

Sometimes an actor simply looking at a space for the first time with eyes of wonder, question, and conflict can give birth to the necessary movements. Remember the saying, a picture says a thousand words? The director and DP are thinking in pictures; just give them something to look at. A collaboration of this kind could be a turning point in the film; a revelation of character and an insight to the whole story. If the actor is not emotionally prepared to meet the terms of this moment, than it doesn't really matter how it's shot or what the actor does; it will appear thin and unimportant.

Completely on the other side of the spectrum is the reverse situation, which can be just as stunning to the actor. You could be fully emotionally prepared for this scene; you see it as a lovely opportunity to show, in a simple, beautiful way, something about the character and, perhaps, metaphorically speaking, about the whole film. The location of the ballroom in shabby demise thrills you, and your imagination runs wild the moment you see it. You can't wait to get in front of the camera.

However, your director doesn't see the scene this way; the set is just a background to this transitional shot. He sees it as being quick and clear. Zina enters, she's tired, she sits down alone, and puts her head in her hands—we never really see her face—beat, and cut. This can be frustrating for an actor. It is the reverse of the above, but the same rules apply—use the here and now and play the moment. Again, your expectations have not been met, and you feel frustrated. That would be appropriate for the playing of this scene as envisioned by the director. The key to using your preparation in any film situation is the transformation of the personal truth to the immediate requirements of the moment in the scene. Give in to the situation, stay relaxed, and stay in the moment.

In the rare event, an actor can change the mind of a director if the DP sees things the same way you do. But you have to be very careful here. You never want to give the director the feeling that you are trying to direct his movie. That will cause tremendous problems. However, a director can be inspired and suddenly see things in a certain way that illuminates his own ideas. Most directors say that they want a cast and crew who will constantly inspire them. They say that they dream of such moments. The truth is that when it does happens—when true inspiration comes from some other source and is contrary to the director's original vision—under the pressures of shooting, only the truly great directors are able to be open to it. You never know how your director will react until the moment presents itself.

There is a myriad of possibilities of what might occur on a film set; I have presented just a few of them. The reality is that nobody, not the director or the producer, let alone the actor, can predict what will happen when everyone is assembled to work on shooting the movie. The actors, who are ultimately what we see in the finished film, are often thought to be responsible for many things over which they have absolutely no control. But film is a collaborative art, with each bringing his or her share to the table, and it takes a skilled, experienced eye to untangle the net of who is responsible for the way a film turns out. No matter who is truly responsible, it is always the director's fault, since he is the commander in chief of the whole affair.

Once the shooting of your part is done, you go home, as the work on the film continues in postproduction. The next time you see your work could be at the premiere or at a special screening for the cast and crew. The final result could leave you very surprised, for better or for worse. In special situations, actors are allowed to see the dailies, and this is yet another can of worms if you aren't used to seeing yourself, warts and all, so to speak. In the next chapter, I will talk about what you can learn about your acting from seeing yourself on the screen and how to make it positively affect your future work as an actor, whether you like the results or not.

THE RUSHES AND THE FINISHED FILM

There is a dream you have when you act in films, a dream of an image of yourself on the screen—a you that is larger-than-life and encompasses a message or a feeling that you are compelled to express. Sometimes, it is a very clear image in your mind; sometimes, it is just a shadow or a glimmer of something that you reach to understand. It could be a part of yourself that you long to embrace or a part of yourself that you wish to expel, to exorcise. Whichever it is, this dream image may or may not show up on the screen when you first see yourself acting in film. The pursuit of that image can cause you to keep coming back again and again to work before the camera, always searching for the satisfaction of some desire of seeing yourself in a projected image, and by seeing that image, you hope to learn who you are.

When you are first starting out, I believe you are searching for something about yourself that you believe you will find in your projected image. That image will show you something that heretofore only existed, many times as a mystery, intimately inside yourself. Coming to terms with what that message is, and what it isn't, is the revelation and the disappointment of watching yourself act in a projected image.

THE RUSHES

The term "rushes" comes from the fact that the lab rushes a print out in one night for the director and crew to view their day's work on the next day. The print is rough; it isn't perfect. Sometimes it's silent or the sound is of bad quality and certainly not mixed correctly. The labs have small screening rooms, where everyone topples in after a long day's shooting, usually in an exhausted state. Again, the gears shift from the activity of doing to the concentration of watching and accessing.

The director and DP must watch the rushes, or dailies (both terms are used interchangeably), to make sure that what they thought they were capturing during shooting is actually arriving onto the screen. Each department head will be present, each only looking at the work for which his department is responsible. The set decorator looks at the set, the makeup artist at the makeup, the gaffer watches the lights, along with the DP and director, who are watching everything. All of the takes that were requested to be printed of each shot, identified by their slate, will be viewed in succession and scrutinized. Choices will be made and unmade and then made again; the editor will take notes. It is an atmosphere of intense concentration, as everyone goes back over what has been shot and decides what has worked, what to reshoot, and how to proceed.

It could be an atmosphere of relief and elation if things are going well and the movie is starting to emerge. Or it could be an atmosphere of tense depression if it starts to become clear that what everyone thought was crystal clear during shooting has not made it to the screen. At the end of the day, the camera doesn't lie. At this point in the process, only the director and the DP truly know what they intended to accomplish in each shot and if any of the takes serves that purpose.

A piece of film does not exist in a vacuum; it must fit into what goes before it and what comes after it. A take can be wonderful in and of itself, but if it doesn't work in the succession of images that it is supposed to be a part of, if it doesn't fit into its planned purpose in the movie, then it cannot be used. The continuity, the timing, all technical concerns, and the dramatic event must coincide with the vision of the completed film. Many films change radically once their rushes are viewed—a director could realize that something else is emerging before him, something other than he had realized was possible. He might decide to alter his future plans to accommodate this new aspect to the story. It can be a wonderfully creative experience in the best-case scenario, or it can spell disaster and confusion if what emerges as the rushes cannot be woven into the fabric of the finished movie.

THE ACTOR AND THE RUSHES

Viewing rushes for an actor is an acquired taste, and many actors do not want to see the rushes at all. They feel it makes their performance too self-conscious. Many, however, especially stars, demand it and have the right to be present written into their contracts. They want to maintain quality control over their work and voice their opinions about the direction the film is taking. Only stars of great popular value can place themselves in such a position.

Besides, a lot of directors feel that an actor has no place at dailies. They feel that seeing the daily footage only bruises the actor's ego and takes away from the power of the director to control or manipulate the performance. Depending on the actor, this can turn out to be true, and if it is true, and the actor sees the rushes anyway, it can cause problems on the set in the subsequent days of shooting. The general rule on most movies is, *no actors at the rushes.* Of course, there are exceptions to every rule, and every actor/director relationship is different. The director might ask you to attend the dailies or you could ask permission on your own. You just might be granted the privilege.

So, why would you want to go to the rushes, if you have no decision-making power in the progress of the movie? There are several reasons. First of all, you can benefit a great deal from watching multiple takes of your work and becoming accustomed to what you look like on the screen. If you don't have a highly developed relationship with the image of yourself on the screen, it can eventually become detrimental, even crippling to your future in film acting. Sometimes you envision yourself as being completely different than what your image turns out to be. I am not talking about your technique now; I'm simply talking about your film presence and what it conveys.

The first time I saw myself acting on the screen, I had a strange feeling that is difficult to describe. It was like suddenly seeing someone up close that I had only previously observed from afar—like meeting a familiar stranger. It was like falling in love with someone with whom loving is forbidden, and yet knowing in that same moment that I would allow myself to fall. It's hard to admit it so blatantly, but I fell in love with myself, or rather the self that I could see moving within the image on the screen, a self that I had only had a glimpse of before, never knowing for sure if it was really there. And now seeing it, before me on the screen, was like opening up a door that would change my life forever. It was the beginning of a fleeting love affair that I was about to pursue, and just like any other relationship of such an intense nature, it would be beset with care, nurturing, and land mines.

This relationship with the self comes with the territory of acting. Like any lasting relationship, it requires attention and skill to keep alive and healthy. Viewing the rushes of your work in a film can be (if you choose to see them in the first place) an excellent tool to bettering your work, as long as you can see yourself in the right frame of mind. The same technique of assessing your work that should follow any exercise work should now be employed to assess what you see in your work in the rushes. It's a wonderful opportunity, because you see yourself repeating the same actions and scenes over and over again, but with the added advantage that you can learn to be an observer of your work, detached from yourself. You can learn to be objective, at least to some degree.

To develop the skill of objective, constructive observation of your screen image, you must first accept what it is and hopefully, as occurred with me, love—in the most positive sense of the word—this image. This doesn't mean that you egotistically become involved with your looks or that you become enraptured and enthralled. It means that through an acceptance of what you are projecting, you can clear the slate. This enables you to constructively criticize you own work. Without this loving acceptance, it is very difficult to be a film actor at all and nearly impossible to assess your acting work.

ASSESSING YOUR WORK IN THE RUSHES

In chapter 12, I mentioned that one of the advantages of doing a student film is being allowed to view the rushes or the rough cut of the film. One of the disadvantages with student films is that their technical quality is often not up to a professional level, and you might not have been photographed, so to speak, in your best light. It could be hard to assess yourself from a technical point of view if you haven't been lit properly or there isn't enough coverage of the scene for you to see your acting work fully. You won't encounter this problem in professional films as a rule. Assessing your work in the context of the whole film becomes a possibility when how a scene is lit and covered is intentional and not the result of lack of experience.

Whatever the level or style of the film dailies that you are viewing, there is a way to break down your observations so that they can be specific and creatively constructive. Believe it or not, the best place to start is with the relaxation and the face.

THE FACE

The first thing to look for is the harboring of tension in the face. Watch your face and ask yourself the following questions:

- Is there a blinking or fluttering of the eyes, particularly in close-up?
  Tension in the eye area causes this problem, and you will quickly see why it should be eliminated; it's very distracting on the screen. It's easy to underestimate how much pressure you're feeling when you act on a set, especially as the camera comes in closer to your face. The problem of blinking could simply be that you didn't pay as much conscious attention to your relaxation as you should have while you were working. Another reason could be that you avoided something about the moment, that you didn't meet it head-on, that you weren't direct. Being direct when you act in front of the camera isn't a character trait; it's a commitment to the dramatic

moment.

- Is there any part of the face that twitches or seems frozen?

This is the same tension problem as the previous example. Tension is being harbored in some area of the face. You can notice it in the corners of the mouth, the eyebrows, or the position of the chin. It is caused by not paying attention to the relaxation process while acting and not meeting the moment head-on.

- Are you camera shy? Do you turn your head in the wrong direction for the camera to see what is happening on your face?

It's a strange phenomenon, but many outgoing and charismatic people can be camera shy; it turns up in the most unlikely places. Sometimes, it's just a lack of experience that causes you to move in a way that is not, photographically speaking, your best choice. The general rule is, if you can see the lens, the lens can see you, and when you act in two shots, mediums, or wider, you have many options of movement. When you watch the rushes, see if you are always moving your head in a way that looks natural in the scene, yet shows the expression of your face.

- Are you utilizing the light to the best of your advantage?

It takes a bit of practice, but certainly, acting in film is finding the best way to optimize the light without anyone noticing that you are doing it. Moving your face a quarter of an inch can make all the difference in the world. This works together with not being camera shy. The camera must be able to see your face. To develop this skill, I would suggest going to museums and looking at the painting of the old masters, like Rembrandt, Vermeer, and Caravaggio. A painting is like one film frame, and studying how these painters constructed meaning with light will help you to understand the possibilities when you act within the moving images of film frames.

- When we see your eyes, are they in focus and looking at something, or do you stare blankly?

If your eyes are blank, it means that you have spaced out in that moment, there's nothing happening internally, and unless that is the goal of that specific moment, like you're dead or a zombie or something like that, something should always be happening in your eyes. Just as you should have the ability to stare, with expressive eyes, without blinking, you should also have the ability to move the eyes in any direction without blinking. Bette Davis was a master at this, and although that highly melodramatic style of acting is no longer in fashion, it's fun to watch her for her eye technique.

- When you see your face on the screen, do you become obsessed with the way you look?

  This is an important issue, because vanity gone awry can destroy an actor. We all have physical characteristics that we are unhappy with, but when you watch the rushes, don't get involved with the aspects of yourself that you hate. Many times nature has given you these traits to enhance the uniqueness of your face. The very thing that you despise might be your best asset, because when it comes purely to looks; we are often the worst judges of ourselves. Remember that what you dislike about your looks may be the very traits that got you the job in the first place. Accept how you feel about your looks and move on, back to focusing on the things that you can change about your performance.

THE BREATH AND THE VOICE

When you watch your work in the rushes, it is very easy to see how one breath can change the intensity of a shot and make it stand out from all the other takes. The way an actor breathes or doesn't breathe is very obvious on film, if you are looking for it. If the breath is not fulfilling the emotional needs of the moment, the actor looks wooden. Whether an outside or internal impulse causes you to breathe appropriately for the moment or if just simply remembering to breathe causes you to connect to the impulse is determined by each individual acting instrument. For many actors, it works both ways, depending on the circumstances. Checking the breath should be an automatic part of any film acting technique.

Along with the breath, of course, comes the voice. Does your voice sound stagy? If it does, then all but absolutely necessary dialogue will end up on the cutting room floor. Nothing kills a movie performance quicker than a wooden or stagelike voice. Of course, we all know the cadre of great British character actors who play in movies all the time and fill them with their booming voices. The ones who do this consistently are usually playing fairy tale figures, inhumans, or superhumans. It's a certain niche that uses this stagelike voice to create a fantasy world. In other words, it's not realistic. Most movie acting is realistic in style and, therefore, requires a more relaxed approach. The British character actors, when they are not playing superheroes and witches, adjust their vocal production to a more natural vein, at least those of them who can.

On the other hand, you might be devoicing at inappropriate moments, which is again a problem of not meeting the dramatic moment head-on.

There is usually some aspect of the character, or the scene, that you haven't properly investigated, and it causes you to falter in your voice. It could be that you haven't found the courage to meet this moment head-on and commit to revealing what it is that you have found in your investigative process. One of the great benefits to watching the rushes is that you quickly see how backing down from the moment weakens your performance. Rather than experience regret or anger at yourself for not having done what you know you are capable of doing, learn from the experience and garner the courage for the next time around. It becomes easier with each try.

THE BODY

Moving and placing your body is often unnatural in film acting. In order to make body positions appear natural in the camera frame, they often become strange, tension-producing configurations. It's an unfortunate hazard of the craft that must be mastered. No matter how abnormal your body position is, it has to look right for the moment it is portraying in the shot. When you watch repeated takes of yourself doing the same thing over and over again, take notice of the following:

- Are you harboring tension somewhere in your body that can be seen in the camera frame?

- Is your fatigue or discomfort more visible with each take? In other words, do you get more strained rather than more relaxed each time you repeat?

Take as an example the athletes and dancers who continue to perform with excellence and aplomb, even though their muscles are screaming or feet are aching. You would never know from their performance that they are in pain or discomfort; you never see it. As an actor, you have to develop the same ability. Ideally, your acting should get better with each take, not worse.

- Is there any way that you can transform the tension creatively? Can you release it into an impulse, put it into your performance, and fill out the life of your character?

Sometimes, the tension that occurs in the body is a suppressed impulse. If you were to identify the tension in the body and release it, it could illuminate something in the scene, bring something fresh to the moment, or create the unexpected. This is what you are looking for in film acting—using the release of tension to uncover new ground—not being relaxed to the point of being limp. Of course, you must do it in a way that stays within the camera frame, adheres to your blocking, and is appropriate to the scene. This takes experience and practice. The exercises in Mental Relaxation and concentration are the training ground for transforming the impulse constructively in a professional situation.

- Is the body presence alive? When you see all or some of your body, along with your head, is it acting, too?

    The body is a huge, intelligent playing field for an actor, but the constricting nature of some camera setups can make you forget that you even have a body, especially if you have been doing a lot of work focusing on the mid-chest and up. If this appears to be a problem, you might consider using an Overall for the character in the wider shots. This would expand the sensory response and spring the body into action. Remember, the key to using any sense memory in a professional situation is to have worked on it thoroughly beforehand. It could spell disaster if mid-movie, you decide to switch horses and throw in a technique that you have never worked on or have little experience with. Besides, it gives sense memory a bad name.

YOUR ACTING PREPARATION AND PERFORMANCE

Preparing for a role can be very exciting and enjoyable if you love to act— in fact, I know many actors who would rather prepare than perform a role. Needless to say, their careers suffer from this tendency. The only real test of a preparation is how it plays out in the performance. Except for the intimate pages of your own journal and perhaps a loving teacher, no one cares about what you had intended your performance to be; they only care about what they can see. When you watch the rushes, you must be aware of how much of your intention is up there on the screen. It takes an objective, intelligent eye to judge this correctly, but because none of us can be completely objective about ourselves, you have to rely on the comments of your director. If he likes what you are doing, then you should keep doing it; if he doesn't like it, then you will have to change something. Since you are the only one who truly knows what your preparation is, you are the only one who can fix it.

There is another scenario where the director likes what you have been doing, but you are not satisfied with your work; you expected something more from yourself. If this is the case, you should assess your work from a technical rather than interpretive point of view.

- Are you completely concentrated in the scene and listening to the other actors?

- Is your sensory work or any other kind of preparation you have chosen obvious? It shouldn't be; it should be completely invisible.

- Are you being self-indulgent instead of being in the moment? By the time you get to the set to work, everything that you do must be anchored into the script and the driving actions of the scene. If something makes you feel engaged and concentrated, but it doesn't work for the script, it must be discarded.

- Are you reaching for a better performance with each take, or do you lose the ability to concentrate as the takes progress? Do you start to *push* your performance as you get tired? You might have repeated something many, many times, but with each repetition you should become more confident and more relaxed.

- Are you able to create as if for the first time with each repetition? This is very important, since your best acting take could have camera difficulties and therefore be unusable. One hears about the first take being the best for many actors because they are fresh with discovery, but very few shots are gotten on the first take— you must be able to successively repeat.

- Does your work match and make sense for the character from the master through to the close-ups?

- Are you revealing more intimate details of the character as the camera comes in closer?

If you are truly unhappy with your work, you won't have the power to reshoot something unless the director and DP want to do it as well; but you do have the power to adjust your future performance. You have to be very careful when making any major decisions about this though. Take your cue from the name of the thing that you are viewing, the rushes, and don't rush into any big decisions about how you look or how to change your performance. You can't change horses in midstream, especially if everyone thinks that you've got a great horse to begin with. You can't suddenly go mutinous and start directing yourself in your own little movie. That's why directors don't want actors at the rushes to begin with; they think they'll go native and be lost in the jungle of their own ideas.

If there is something about your work that bothers you, then speak to the director about it to find out how and if it needs to be fixed. If the director assures you that you're doing great and to just keep up the good work, then, whether you agree with him or not, you'll have to do as he says, or at least try to. Hopefully, you will learn a great deal from watching yourself, and the experience will enrich the rest of your performance, as well as your future roles. You might even find yourself enjoying the process.

THE FINISHED FILM

In most cases, as I mentioned before, the actors are not permitted to see the rushes. This means that the first time that you see your work will be after all of the postproduction work is completed, in the finished film. The best way for this to happen is at a special cast-and-crew screening. Everyone in the audience has worked on or been associated with the movie in some way. The atmosphere is always positive.

It is also possible that you see the film for the first time when it is released to the public in a theater, on videocassette, DVD, or broadcast on television. This is a much more difficult situation, because you are without the support of the rest of the cast and crew; you are unprotected from public opinion. If this is the way that you first see your work in a film, I would suggest not seeing it alone; I would see it accompanied by a few good, close friends. If the work is good, you'll want to share it with others, and if it's not, you'll need the support and humor of the people who know and care about you. That's what I always do.

It's easy to underestimate the impact of seeing your work for the first time along with the public, especially if you've never seen any of the rushes. It can be very shocking. It's easy to feel as though you've been manipulated or even deceived. It takes a lot of experience to let go of your desire to influence your character after you have long left the set. You have to keep in mind that although the image looks like you and sounds like you, that image no longer belongs to you; it belongs to the film and the filmmakers. That's part of the deal. However, you can still assess your work, just as you would have done at the rushes, except now, you only have the material that they have chosen to use. You lose the benefit of being able to judge your work in the multiple takes of each shot. You'll never know whether there was a better take that wasn't used for some technical reason or because it didn't match the rhythm of the rest of the scene, or for that matter if you were really awful in all other takes except the one they used. I would suggest just enjoying the movie as a whole at your first viewing, and then going back to assess your work at a later date.

You should be prepared that the context and size of your role might have changed drastically from what you thought it was intended to be. A major role on the set could be reduced to a few minor appearances, or even worse, completely edited out of the movie. You won't be notified of these changes; you'll experience it for the first time when you're sitting in the movie theater with everyone else. An experience like this can be devastating and disappointing. After all the work and anticipation, your work isn't even seen in the film. You have to take this in stride, feel bad for a few minutes, and then focus on your next role.

Everyone who works in film wants the films that they work on to be very good, some even aspire to greatness; nobody wants to make a bad movie. But most people who work in film are anonymous beyond the insular world of the entertainment industry. The actors face a different situation altogether; it is their faces and bodies that are up there on the screen, and everyone knows who they are and what they look like. Actors can take it very hard if their performance is not well-received in a film. It can be very embarrassing. On the other side of the spectrum, if their performance is a success, they can become ecstatic and elated and lose all perspective of their worth. Both situations can cause ego problems in their future work.

All actors have to develop a kind of second skin that protects them, and their work, from outside critical voices, whether they are negative or positive, but for the film actor, it is especially important. Theater actors and their audience share the same space and time together during the performance. When the performance is over, everyone goes home, and the cast returns the next day to perform again. Actors in film share the space and time of their work with the other cast and crew members with no audience present. On almost every film, this group binds together like an extended family, supporting and helping one another through the work. When the shoot is over, this family disbands as the film is prepared for public release. There is no going out with the rest of the cast for a beer and a laugh after a bad performance if the film is ill-received. As a film actor, you are usually left to your own devices when dealing with the disappointments and joys of the public's opinion of your work.

Once again, it's a good time to go back to the relaxation and concentration—to write in your journal and assess the situation—to continue the development of the intimate relationship to the self and how you feel in any given moment in time. Once you admit how you feel in one moment, the moment will change to something else, and on and on it goes eternally. Movies are a part of our collective dreams, and just like the movies of your own memory are a part of you, your work becomes a part of someone else's imagination. Somehow, I feel like we are all together, in an imaginary space, dreaming of a greater understanding of ourselves, reaching for new ideas and solutions that we believe we can find if we work collectively. And we actors of the twenty-first century, we play our parts in this modern drama by exhibiting our faces, our bodies, and our very souls by acting in film.

Here is a list of books that I have read again and again. They have been used as a reference point for this book and serve as a suggested reading list.

Argentini, Paul. *Elements of Style for Screenwriters*. Los Angeles: Lone Eagle, 1998.

Blacker, Erwin R. *The Elements of Screenwriting*. New York: MacMillan, 1996.

Chaiken, Joseph. *The Presence of the Actor*. New York: Atheneum, 1977.

Dougan, Andy. *Martin Scorsese*. New York: Thunder's Mouth Press, 1998.

Hagen, Uta. *Respect for Acting*. New York: MacMillan, 1973.

Hethmon, Robert H. *Strasberg at the Actors Studio*. New York: Theatre Communications Group, 1991.

Horowitz, Marilyn. *How to Write a Screenplay in Ten Weeks*. New York: Artmar, 1999.

Lewis, Robert. *Advice to the Players*. New York: Harper and Row, 1980.

Lumet, Sidney. *Making Movies*. New York: Vintage Press, 1996.

Magarshack, David. *Stanislavsky on the Art of the Stage*. London: Faber Paperbacks, 1950.

Stanislavski, Constantin. *An Actor Prepares*. New York: Routledge, 1989.

Strasberg, Lee. *A Dream of Passion*. New York: Plume, 1988.